END GAME

AS REAL AS IT GETS

CORNEL RIZEA

Copyright © 2021 by Cornel Rizea
All rights reserved.

ISBN: 978-1-7321807-4-1 (print)
ISBN: 978-1-7321807-5-8 (e-book)

Cover and Interior Book Design by Inspire Books
www.inspire-books.com

Scripture quotations marked ESV are taken from the ESV® Bible (The Holy Bible, English Standard Version®), copyright © 2001 by Crossway, a publishing ministry of Good News Publishers. Used by permission. All rights reserved.

Scripture quotations marked BSB are taken from the Holy Bible, Berean Study Bible, BSB. Copyright ©2016 by Bible Hub. Used by Permission. All Rights Reserved Worldwide.

Scripture quotations marked HCSB are taken from the Holman Christian Standard Bible®, Copyright © 1999, 2000, 2002, 2003, 2009 by Holman Bible Publishers. Used by permission. HCSB® is a federally registered trademark of Holman Bible Publishers.

Scripture quotations marked NASB are taken from the New American Standard Bible® (NASB). Copyright © 1960, 1962, 1963, 1968, 1971, 1972, 1973, 1975, 1977, 1995 by The Lockman Foundation. Used by permission. www.Lockman.org.

Scripture quotations marked NLT are taken from the Holy Bible, New Living Translation, copyright ©1996, 2004, 2015 by Tyndale House Foundation. Used by permission of Tyndale House Publishers, Inc., Carol Stream, Illinois 60188. All rights reserved.

I want to dedicate this book to my family, friends, acquaintances, and all those who are willing to honestly humble themselves and aspire to be in heaven one day. It has been the highest honor of my life to write about what really matters. I have been blessed beyond words to be able to share with you the most relevant fantastic news for all of humanity. May God bless you and keep you, today and always!

If anyone wants to reach out to share your story, I can be reached at cornel@rizea-books.com.

You can also find out more at www.rizea-books.com

CONTENTS

Preface vii
Introduction xiii

1. Stop, Look & Listen 1
2. God 11
3. Heaven & Hell 21
4. Chosen to Believe 31
5. Relationships 39
6. All Puffed-Up 49
7. Debt + Doubt = Death 59
8. Left Behind 67
9. Seven-Year Tribulation Period 79
10. 1,000 Years + Eternal State = Forever End Game 91
11. Recognition + Remorse + Repentance = Redemption ... 103

PREFACE

You can't take it with you. That's the expression and underlying theme that came to mind as I was trying to figure out just where exactly I wanted to start this, my third and final book.

When I first contemplated the idea of a third book, I admit that it got a bit overwhelming right off the bat. After all, I had gone through this a couple of times already during the recent past. I knew all too well the time and energy commitment needed to see it through. It's not like I was avoiding it, but like anything else, I needed to put away my excuses and simply begin.

Just as the prior two times, I knew in my heart that this final topic was also extremely important. It matters more than I could possibly express in a few short chapters. As much as I tried to ignore the inner voices to not bother, it was weighing on me to get it out on paper and into the hands of others in my immediate circle of influence. Perhaps it will reach places I cannot even imagine so I wouldn't be surprised if that happened.

I recall how just a few short years ago the idea of writing was nowhere near my bucket list. I certainly didn't expect to be in this position at this time, but here I am. I have just recently retired a mere couple of months ago from my full-time job and feel extremely humbled, blessed, and fortunate from so many points of view. Once again, I'm compelled to share with you what's on my heart, so here we go, one last time.

The one thing I know for sure is that the reason for me to write again remains the same as when I began this journey. Simply put, I'm hopeful that you will benefit from reading this book. That's it in a nutshell. If you're reading these words, I want you to know that it's not too late to prepare for the extreme events yet to come. It's the reason for this third book. I would encourage you to open your heart, dare to expose yourself to brutal honesty, then look through your mind's eye to get a glimpse of what the future has in store. I would like for you to understand how this will impact you personally.

I'm hopeful that you'll gain confidence to take decisive action from a higher level of understanding of the past, the present, as well as the reality of the things yet to come. I'm hopeful that this book will increase your personal comfort level regardless of the exact position you find yourself in at this very moment. I'm hopeful that the fear of the unknown will dissipate quickly like fog when exposed to a sunny morning. I'm hopeful that you will get to experience true inner peace deep within your being regardless of absolutely any future event yet to unfold outside of your control.

Lastly, I'm hopeful that you, in turn, will be in a better position to help someone else and thus pay it forward. Knowing that you've made a positive difference in someone else's life is truly rewarding beyond words. Helping others is really an amazing gift you get to give yourself and I'm hopeful that you will end up looking forward to the future with certainty and assurance.

I began with the statement *you can't take it with you*. So, *what* exactly is it that you can't take with you, you may ask? Well, it's all your stuff. You will not be able to take any of your own possessions with you, nor anyone else's for that matter. Actually, you will not be able to take any of your friends nor any family members either. And *where* exactly is this place where you can't take anything nor anyone else with you? Well, that would be the place where you end up after you die.

It may seem obvious, but if you were to bring up this topic at a cocktail party or a group gathering, you will likely not find many who were willing to engage in this conversation, at least not in any meaningful way. It doesn't seem to be very popular so most simply and mistakenly avoid it at every turn. On the other hand, you might find that others do have varying, although somewhat superficial, opinions about the future things to come and how it will all come to an end. My experience is that most have not given it much consideration at all. Everyone is *too busy*, or so they claim. So, if you're curious and feel compelled to do so, then I would hope that continuing to read further would bring you great value.

Before we dive right into the real meat of the future events, I want to outline for you some prerequisites in the first few chapters that are needed so you can fully appreciate the latter few chapters. It matters and I'm hopeful you will agree once you reach the end of the book. Yes, I can imagine what may be going through your mind right about now. You might be thinking that your future after you die is secure somehow, so why bother worrying about it. More specifically, why bother even talking about it, much less reading about it? After all, you may rightfully reason that you're a good person anyway. Every day, you try your best to do the right thing, you respect others and pretty much mind your own business.

Or you might be thinking that you don't even believe there is anything after you die. You then quickly reason that you will not need anything anyway. After all, you might not believe there is anyone out there after you die. You might be in the camp that this life here and now is all there is. Live it up to the max because tomorrow you may not be here, so you don't want to miss out on what's going on right now.

Or, you might be relatively young, so you could be thinking that your final breath will likely take place one day, many years into the future. No need to spend any time considering and certainly not dwelling on this subject at your young age. You can catch up on the details later, you think to yourself, as you've got lots of time. You may even reason that certainly you will have a chance to make any necessary adjustments needed to adequately prepare at that point. I mean, what's the rush, right?

What if you knew in advance the events of the future things to come with vivid clarity? What if you knew that these future events are not that far away, and they would usher in the final days on earth? What if you were certain about the reality of the final destinations which every living soul faces after death? Do you believe this world will continue moving forward as it always has in the past, or do you believe that it will all end in a grand finale somehow?

If you knew in advance of these future things to come, would you honestly ignore them today, or would you possibly consider them for your future wellbeing? I'm hopeful that you'll take the time to gain understanding about the final *END GAME*. It's *As Real As It Gets*.

INTRODUCTION

Little Johnny was coming of that certain curious age, so he went to his dad one day and began by saying, *dad, where do people come from?* Somewhat surprised but immensely proud, the dad began taking his time explaining to his little boy saying, *well, Johnny, now that you asked, it's called evolution. You see many, many years ago, we started out as apes and slowly over time we became less and less hairy, and we began to walk and to talk and well, here we are now as regular people everywhere.* Johnny then went away scratching his head, trying to wrap his little mind around what he just heard.

That night Johnny was tossing around in bed trying to fall asleep while thinking about his dad's answer relating to apes turning into people. The next morning after his dad was off to work, he went to his mom and asked, *mom, where do people come from?* Now, Johnny's mom stopped what she was doing, sat down next to him and began with, *wow my little boy is growing up!* She then continued by saying, *well, Johnny, now that you* asked, it's called creation. You see, many years ago, it was God from heaven who created a man whose name was Adam and a woman whose name was Eve. The two of them had kids and grandkids and over time there are now many people on earth.

Somewhat confused, Johnny looked at his mother and said to her, *but yesterday I asked dad the same question and he told me that people came from apes.* His mother then patiently smiled and looked at her son saying, *well, don't let that bother you, Johnny. You see, your dad was just talking about his side of the family.*

If you're still chuckling at that *little Johnny* joke, then you pass for having a sense of humor, as far as I'm concerned. Having said that, as funny as some people may think that joke was, others may not be as amused by it. Yes, there are people in the world today who claim that people did evolve from apes. Obviously both scenarios cannot be true and this important difference in thinking should not be overlooked, nor made fun of, nor taken lightly.

This seemingly unassuming starting point regarding where people came from forms the very basis from which every other world event is being viewed and understood by individuals everywhere. Sadly, the end results from these deferring starting points of view are as opposing and as far apart as light is from darkness. I have found that it's the main reason people generally disagree on major issues and principles in life. Sure, individual opinions matter but in the end, what really counts is that we get the starting point right. Otherwise, things seem to fall apart quickly afterwards.

As I'm writing this, it's January 1'st, 2021, so *Happy New*

Year to one and all. Given the unexpected world health pandemic of recent events, the COVID 19 virus epidemic from early 2020, there is no question in anyone's mind that we are living through some unprecedented times. I've also heard others referring to this period using descriptive language such as strange, dangerous, shocking, unique, warped, messed-up and downright weird.

The entire globe was virtually locked down almost as if time stood still for a while, with everyone looking around for answers. Not a single shot got fired nor was there any announcement or warning in advance. *Normal* life was not only interrupted but disrupted in ways unlike any other crisis in world history.

Way too many people lost their lives due to this deadly virus that spread like wildfire across all societies without regard for land borders or oceans. It's been said many times that *today* is certainly a gift, while *tomorrow* is simply not guaranteed to anyone. Indeed, how sobering and true that is.

It was sometime during the onset of this pandemic that I realized I needed to complete this message which was percolating under the surface. Suddenly this current virus event increased my purpose and conviction to get it out as quickly as I could. My desire was to increase awareness, help clarify misunderstandings of future events to come, the conditions necessary prior to their arrival, and perhaps bring about a conversation that needs to be had.

I wanted to write one more time about something that added a sort of bookend to my first two books. I thought that the topic of what the future has in store really mattered in order to complete the big picture. It was important and something that I believed in my heart I needed to do. I wanted to alert others in relatively simple terms and to increase awareness of the reality knocking at the door.

If I were to be totally upfront about it, I was hoping that this final message would resonate and count somehow in the grand picture. Again, I was hoping that it would make a positive difference by helping someone else. The message of this final book has to do with spelling out the future events to come right here on earth as recorded in the Bible. In case you don't already know, these upcoming events are going to be quite terrifying to say the least.

From my personal experience, I found that most people are somewhat curious about the future, but they tend to go to the wrong places to learn about them. It's quite natural to wonder about what may or may not be coming just around the corner. Will the future be bright and bring happiness? Will it be dark and bring sadness and pain? Should we prepare for some hostile invasion from outer space perhaps?

How verse do you think most people are when it comes to the Biblical account for the revealed future things to come? More importantly, how familiar are you with these prophesies? Why should we care? Do you believe they are mere fables, estimated forecasts, or accurate divine revelations? Will mankind and the earth itself survive in the future? If you knew about them in advance, would you even consider the possibility that they could all come true?

This brings us back to the *little Johnny* conversation he had with his mom and dad about where people came from at the beginning of this introduction. Where you personally stand on the topic of evolution or creation matters perhaps more than you realize. It's massive. It's foundational. I mentioned earlier that it forms the basis for how you view everything else, so we must get the beginning right. Do you believe that people evolved from apes? Or do you believe the Biblical account that God, Creator of the entire universe also created Adam and Eve as being the first two people on earth?

It all boils down to whether you believe the words written in the Bible as being true and accurate. That is pretty much it. It boils down to whether you believe that God exists and that He revealed through the various books of the Bible the origin of everything as well as how it will all end. A lot of people say that there is a God, but the question is *do they actually believe it*?

Do you believe that this unique planet we're living on was designed, created, and is being sustained by God Himself? These are all biblical teachings regarding creation. If your answer is *yes* regarding the beginning of everything, then do you believe what the Bible also informs us regarding the future things to come are also true?

What would you think if you learned that the Bible informs us that God Himself is going to destroy this planet at some point in the future? After all, He created it and the claim is that He will be destroying it as well. If it's hard for you to believe that, then you are certainly not alone. If you believe in creation, will you not also believe in the final days as revealed in the Bible? Will you choose to believe that only certain parts of the Bible are true but not others? If so, then how will you determine which parts to believe and which parts to ignore?

I have been fortunate enough to have come across amazing people from all walks of life. It's no surprise to me that some people may or may not believe all of what the Bible has to say. I mean, was there really a time when people lived to be 900 years old? Was the earth flooded at some point with only Noah, his family, and select pairs of animals having survived on a floating ark? Did fire and brimstone actually rain down on Sodom and Gomorrah at God's command? I also found that when it came to future events yet to come, most people wanted to know more as they were simply not sure of the biblical account.

If you ask around how it might end, climate change often comes up among many other topics with serious projected consequences for humanity at large. When I would ask about what they thought of global warming or whether the earth will continue to exist in the future, I heard a variety of opinions. These ranged from massive water levels rising across the globe due to the melting of ice caps, to no significant changes at all. As far as the earth continuing to exist in the future, most had no reason to believe otherwise. The overwhelming response was that things would likely continue to move forward indefinitely. *Who knows*, was an exceedingly popular answer as well.

Granted, I also came across individuals who have not given the future much thought at all. They were too busy being caught up in the day-to-day stuff. I can certainly understand that. Having been around the block a few times myself, so to speak, I have come to a point in my life where I wanted to put this in writing while I am able, all in an effort to help others. I wanted to write about the sequence of future things to come as revealed in the Bible. I also wanted to challenge you to think for yourself with the hope that you too will come to believe the coming events to be true as well.

I am hoping that this message will stir up that certain something within as you continue reading the following chapters. My desire is for you to listen for that inner voice calling you to consider them and to believe. At the same time, if you find yourself being skeptical along the way, I will simply encourage you to continue moving forward to the very end of the book before making up your mind. If you still want to learn what the Bible has to say about future events to come and about the signs that we can all look for in advance, then I am hopeful that you will be better equipped by the end of this message.

I've heard it being said that life is like a math class. Sometimes we add and we subtract. Other times we multiply and divide. Oftentimes we make mistakes, and we would like to make corrections, or we might even prefer to start over. However, the reality is that we simply run out of time. The truth is that the bell rings and math class is over at that point.

I challenge you to care enough and prepare ahead of time while math class is still in session.

CHAPTER 1

Stop, Look & Listen

You might have heard the expression *think for yourself* many times and that's certainly sound advice. It probably comes as no surprise that if asked, most people will quickly assert that they obviously think for themselves. I mean, you don't typically hear someone say something like *no, I'd prefer that someone else think for me*. I will also say upfront that I am by no means referring to nor undermining the unfortunate reality of individuals in our society who suffer from some sort of mental illness and need our help. Thinking for yourself, however as you will find moving forward throughout the book, will be a recurring theme.

You might have also heard that all kinds of experiments and studies of the human brain as well as our subconscious behaviors have been done, likely continuing to this day. After all, these are important as our brain is our onboard computer and it needs to function properly for our wellbeing. For the most part, these studies were conducted in order to understand how to treat or operate or help improve the lives of people in general. At the same time, it would be naive for us to discount the negative impact which the study results revealed as well. People's way of thinking and personal opinions can be altered depending on the information being presented, how it is being disclosed, as well as what information is being withheld on purpose.

Over time, it has been shown through studies of psychology and alike, that people's behaviors may be influenced in various ways. Another realistic, yet even more sinister outcome is that some people may use this to manipulate others in ways that they were not even aware of. Human nature is being exploited in every way possible. We are constantly being bombarded with all kinds of satisfaction surveys, advertisements, and information from various angles, some purposely designed to have the mass population think and behave in a certain way regarding a variety of topics.

The main message in the preceding three paragraphs is for you to personally investigate any subject you choose with a healthy dose of skepticism and to simply *think for yourself*. You want to prevent being drawn into some form of group think just for the sake of going with the flow so as not to ruffle any feathers. Go ahead and take on the responsibility of researching the subject for yourself in order to solidify your foundation to make better informed decisions that will benefit you.

There is certainly some truth in the expression *knowledge is power*. I have often said that once you know the truth, that's all that matters. Once you have knowledge of the truth regarding a subject, your power comes from knowing that truth deep inside of you, regardless of what anyone else may say. It's paramount to look at an issue from all sides without bias. So, go ahead and review all the relevant data available; the good, the bad, and the ugly. Take note of the ways in which the information is being presented, and always consider the source. You will then be best equipped to move forward from that point with what makes most sense to you. You will also have the confidence to be able to defend your position or change it if additional true facts are revealed.

With all that in mind, we'll begin with the main question *creation or evolution?* Only one can possibly be true. This subject is the starting point and its relevance to everything that follows cannot be overstated. I have already mentioned that we must get this right before proceeding. Let's start by considering to simply stop, to look and to listen to nature all around us by focusing on the realities of four true observations.

1. There is the mystery of the many constant forces of nature that currently exist and must remain that way in our universe. The speed of light, gravity, the distance from the sun, the moon orbit, the tilt of the vertical axis of the earth, and the temperature at which water boils at sea level are only a few such constant forces and observations. Evolution proposes that all of these necessary constants became this way *coincidentally* by mere chance.

Science proves these constant forces exist, but science does not explain how they originated with their current exact values, nor why they are not changing. If these constants were to deviate in value by the smallest minute fraction of a fraction of a fraction, renowned cosmologist Stephen Hawking mentioned in his book *A Brief History of Time*, that there would then be no universe and thus no life.

I would draw your attention to the Anthropic principle for the statistical probability of the cosmos and theories of the universe to be just so. Our very existence on this tiny planet along with that of the vast universe depend on the very existence and fine-tuning of all these precise constants of nature. This continuously puts atheists and evolutionists on the defense with no explanation offered. The universe shows complexity and rationality because these are two of the characteristics of the Creator who made it that way. Creationists believe that the best explanation for the existence of the exact constants of nature was part of that intelligent design by the same intelligent designer, God.

2. There is the mystery around the depth of human depravity. Wild animals kill other animals out of necessity to eat because of hunger. You do not see them trying to wipe out the entire species of their food source, much less their own species. Evolution presumes cruelty at all levels of life, but it seems that in the animal kingdom it is tempered by necessity. How does one begin to explain the horrific history of human behavior against other human beings that far exceeds necessity and reaches evil depths that seem unfathomable? The Creationists believe that there are unspeakable depths of human depravity because of the constant struggles between forces of good and evil. There is a biblical account for that.

3. There is the mystery around the existence of human

morality which evolutionists cannot account for. These are not necessarily heroic deeds but even the simple things like helping a neighbor in need, volunteering to clean up after a disaster, bringing food to the needy, providing a shoulder to cry on, or donating blood all because it's the right thing to do. These moral acts cannot be explained by those who think we evolved and are merely programmed to survive and reproduce. Creationists believe that we feel a moral obligation to help others even if it may sometimes work against us. This is because there is a moral law giver, God, who designed us this way in His likeness.

4. Perhaps most importantly, there is the mystery around the existence of the living cell needed for all life here on earth. How did it get here? Who or what was its origin? Many books and scientific articles have been written on the subject. The living cell is extraordinarily complex and has been likened to a sort of supercomputer. Evolution does not explain the original presence of any life form on our planet, much less that of a single living functioning complex cell.

Before one cell can evolve or transition into another cell, there has to be the presupposition that one such living cell existed in the first place. Some evolutionists have even suggested that perhaps aliens from some other planet may have brought the original living cell right here on earth to explain its origin. Creationists believe the best explanation for the origin and existence of the complex living cell structure was intelligently designed this way by an intelligent designer, God Himself.

So, what do you personally think? Which do you believe is more likely? Creation or evolution? The creationist explanation is that God exists. The atheist / evolutionist argues that God does not exist. From reviewing the apparent evidence, it is my humble view that the God explanation does a whole lot better. If we were to stop, look, listen and just consider the existence of this invisible God, then all these observable true facts make sense.

It was the gargantuan importance of getting the genesis of all things right that I originally embarked on writing my first book a few years ago. It is my humble opinion that the vast majority of the problems encountered in the world today, including the ugliness of racism exhibited throughout history, are all a direct result of the lack of belief in the truth about creation and where we all came from.

The entire human race, regardless of the color of skin, points right back to Adam and Eve as ancestors. They were the first two human beings on planet earth, as the pinnacle of God's creation from the very beginning of time. Subsequent generations of people everywhere, all originated from Adam and Eve. To put it bluntly, evolution is the single greatest lie ever told, cleverly disguised to deceive the masses across the globe. Unfortunately, this deception is being perpetuated to this very day among many.

The thought of writing was certainly scary when I began my first book *CITIZEN OF HEAVEN - No Waiting Period Required*, then again, similar emotions for my second book *BEGIN FROM WHERE YOU ARE - Enough With The Excuses*. As of late, just as in the prior two times, I have been bombarded with ideas and the strong belief regarding publishing one more book regarding the end times. Yes, it's still a bit scary even the third time.

Everything seemed to be pointing this way as I felt the increasing sense of needing to complete the final message. I was even jokingly sharing with my wife that this last book was completing a sort of trilogy I was meant to get out there from the start but didn't realize it until later. The only way I can explain the situation I find myself in now is that the picture that's been on my heart to share with you is not yet complete. Hence, this final book *END GAME - As Real As It Gets.*

I started out writing *CITIZEN OF HEAVEN* with a basic message I felt was so important, that it was literally beyond measure. Everyone, perhaps more accurately, *most of us,* would like to end up in heaven after we take our last breath here on earth. The beginning of this journey to heaven boiled down to where each of us stood on the subject of *Creation* vs *Evolution.* One is true, while the other is false. How did it all start? Where did we all come from? We had to get the genesis right.

This critical point is at the root of how someone views, understands, and accepts the origins of all humanity, the earth, and all that exists in the entire universe. As such, where each person stands on how it all came into existence, shapes our individual views of all the things that have ever been recorded in history, how we process what we observe today in society at large, as well as what the future end times have in store for each of us after we die.

Essentially, in order to become a citizen of heaven, it begins with the belief by faith that *In the beginning, God created the heavens and the Earth* (Genesis 1:1). I went into a lot more straight forward, plain to see, common sense, easy to understand detail, but essentially this was the main message of that first book. This was the first step. This belief in supernatural creation by a supernatural God was foundational to understanding everything that followed that remarkable event. It marked the very beginning of human history. It is at the forefront of prerequisites for someone ending up in heaven after life on earth ends.

I made the argument that if Charles Darwin, who is credited with the theory of evolution, had the advantages of modern-day science and DNA discoveries during the past 150 years, then his views on the origin of life would have been vastly different from the ones he penned in 1859. My conclusion was summarized below.

> *No scientist on planet earth can create a single living molecule from a bunch of nonliving chemical compounds, not even while trying to do so deliberately in the most controlled laboratory environment. It is impossible for a living molecule to come into existence by mere chance, irrespective of time.*

I also claimed that if supernatural creation, the origin of all that exists, was misinterpreted or misunderstood or just plain rejected, then all subsequent current and future events would be viewed through very misleading tainted glasses. Once we know where we came from and how we got here, then the vision of the future clears up quickly. The journey toward acquiring citizenship to heaven begins with the belief in supernatural creation. That's where the path to citizenship to heaven starts.

By the word of the Lord the heavens were made, and all the host of them by the breath of His mouth. (Psalm 33:6)

By faith we understand that the worlds were framed by the word of God, so that the things which are seen were not made of things which are visible. (Hebrews 11:3)

The main message of my second book, BEGIN FROM WHERE YOU ARE has to do with moving forward in life without making excuses, regardless of your starting point. I went over what I coined the B.O.W. process (Believe, Observe, Will) in sequential progression toward improvement in any area of life. I used personal examples where I believed things could get better, I observed and learned what was necessary to make improvements, then I had to be willing to apply the lessons learned to make constructive changes and move forward.

By the grace of God, one's life on earth has value, purpose, significance, and meaning. Thinking for yourself matters because you're accountable for every thought, every spoken word and every deed. Believing that God exists matters, and this is the beginning of wisdom. What you personally believe as being the genesis of the universe and all life form matters. The light in which you live your life here on earth matters. Believing the reality of the future events to come, and how they will affect you personally also matters. I'm hopeful that you will be better prepared by getting a glimpse into the **END GAME: As Real As It Gets.**

Biblical Truth from Chapter #1

The entire universe, the earth, and all life form came into existence by supernatural creation.

What do you personally think because it matters? Do you believe it was creation or evolution as the explanation for the genesis of all that is in existence today? Have you done the research for yourself? Are you willing to write it down and put your name on it?

Where you stand on this subject is more important than you realize because it is the foundation upon which all other true observations are built. God is a supernatural being beyond our understanding and He created all that exists. Knowing this brings confidence, comfort, and the assurance of being spared from the devastation of the future things to come.

CHAPTER 2

God

I was searching for an appropriate place to begin this massively important chapter, so I'll start by recalling a time about 15 years ago when I participated in a weekly Bible study group. A small group of guys would meet on Monday nights for about an hour or so. The leader of the group, Ken, was a good friend to all of us and he hosted the group meetings at his house. We all respected his knowledge of biblical doctrine, and this was a place where we all had the chance to talk openly about many subjects.

We got together on a weekly basis to share individual stories, support one another through various situations we were each experiencing during that time, while also learning and growing in our understanding of biblical teachings. The truth is that we also looked forward to the fresh pastries Ken's wife would treat us with at the end of the evening. Thank you for the goodies Fawn. Thy were both delicious and appreciated.

At one of these Monday night Bible study get-togethers, I recall Ken began by asking the question, *how would you describe God or what is He?* After looking at each other for a few seconds, one by one we each rattled off the first thing that came to our minds. While we were coming up with many of God's attributes, Ken continued to challenge us to think of the simplest of terms to describe Him. After waiting patiently for us to exhaust our ideas and not discounting anything we came up with, Ken then made the following statement.

God is a spirit

This simple declaration stuck with me ever since so I'll start this chapter here. I will also mention right up front that if we were to turn all of the existing trees from all forests on planet earth into paper, then use every single sheet of paper to write on both sides in fine print a complete description of God, we would have only just begun this insurmountable task. I mean, how and where does one even begin to provide an all-encompassing total description of an infinite being? God has no beginning and no end. He is everlasting. He has always existed in eternity past and will continue to exist in eternity future.

Although we've come a long way as a civilized society from many points of view, all we need to do is turn on the news to conclude that we, as human beings, still have a long way to go. Entire nations seem to be on vastly different pages when it comes to merely coexisting peacefully right here on planet earth. There is certainly enough space for everyone so what seems to be the problem? Why are so many people on the proverbial edge despite the giant leaps forward in living standards experienced during the most recent centuries?

We're now actively pursuing the possibility of moving to other planets just to get away from each other. It's a bit funny when you hear jokes about cars that were only invented so we can one day ship them to the moon or Mars, pick up girls, or guys, then drive around up there for a while. After all, we could use some variety around here. We're just not that satisfied with all that this planet earth has to offer. Maybe life will be better up there in outer space somewhere. Maybe people will behave differently wearing space suits. Oh, and let's not forget that we still need to work out the minor details for the outhouse sanitation system too.

Unfortunately, throughout all of humanity, very few people seem to pay attention to history books that are filled with numerous examples of what not to do. Instead, generation after generation across the globe seem to have an insatiable desire for more and more control. Whether anyone admits it or not, whether anyone likes it or not, the main problem is not the color of one's skin, it is the devastating effect of sin. The main problem with most people is godlessness. To state the obvious, all human beings are clearly flawed with a fallen nature, and we do not naturally gravitate toward a holy God.

Just look around and think about it for a moment. The wild animal kingdom has always been intriguing to us humans, and for good reason. They do their thing day in and day out, although it sometimes looks brutal when it comes to what they have to deal with in order to survive. Observing it all take place on land or in the air or in the sea is quite remarkable to say the least.

On the human side, people all over the globe are busy working, walking, talking, playing, sleeping, having kids and so on. You might have noticed that there has always been a whole lot of arguing and disagreeing going on as well. However, for the most part, life just happens everywhere. Sure, we all have individual concerns and goals, but we do our best to make ends meet and move forward. For the most part, we want to live and let live, then retire one day and perhaps enjoy the golden years. It's the circle of life. Hakuna matata.

When contemplating it all, the following questions are very personal but worth considering.

- Do you think this is all there is?
- Do you think there is a bigger purpose behind it all?
- Do you think all people have a chance to survive going forward?
- If God is the author of creation, do you think this is how He intended for it to be?
- Do you think it will all come to an end and if so, how?
- Do you think we will be given warnings first and do you know what to look for?

Throughout this third and final book, I will do my best to challenge you to think for yourself. I will also do my absolute best to be straight up and not sugar coat things. My intention is to bring up some topics in the way in which I'd want to receive them if our roles were reversed, always in honesty and love. When it will really matter, your personal convictions cannot be overstated. Your peace of mind and happiness completely depend on your personal beliefs and assurances.

From the opening first chapter, if you landed on the side of Creation by the one and only true God as the genesis for everything, then congratulations because that's correct. Given all that is obvious and given all that we know from scientific observation, Supernatural Creation is the most likely cause for the existence of all that we see. As I mentioned earlier, we need to get the beginning right. It all starts with that as a solid foundation on which to build further. Yes, it takes faith to believe in Creation, however it makes a whole lot more sense than the foolish idea of mere chance.

> *The fool says in his heart, "There is no God." (Psalm 14:1)*
>
> *In the beginning God created the heavens and the earth. (Genesis 1:1)*
>
> *The heavens declare the glory of God; the skies proclaim the work of His hands. (Psalm 19:1)*
>
> *Through Him all things were made; without Him nothing was made that has been made. (John 1:3)*
>
> *For since the creation of the world God's invisible qualities – His eternal power and divine nature – have been clearly seen, being understood*

> *from what has been made, so that people are without excuse.* (Romans 1:20)

All forms of matter and all forms of life originated from a supernatural God speaking everything into existence. We, as human beings will never understand exactly how that can be possible because we're mortal. The supernatural, immortal, one and only true God made it happen just so. We, the people of this unique planet earth are the pinnacle of His creation made in His image.

Although I mentioned at the beginning of this chapter that no person can possibly provide a total and complete description of God, we certainly know enough to put our faith and trust in Him.

God is truth. It's His nature. It's His essence. The one thing God cannot do is lie. He has communicated to us humans through Creation itself, and through divine inspiration via the Holy Bible, God's word, for our own good.

God is eternal. He is a supernatural being. He is not bound by time nor anything else. He has always existed in eternity past and will continue to exist in eternity future. There is nothing else that preceded Him, nor will there be anything after Him.

God is holy. Known as the Holy Trinity, God the Father, God the Son, and God the Holy Spirit are distinct yet each perfectly Holy God. Together, they make up the one true triune God of the universe. Being holy is also His nature and essence unlike anything else in existence. He is the one and only true God, perfect to the highest order possible, and completely set apart on every level. He is without comparison to anything or anyone else in existence since He is the Creator of all that exists. He alone is divine and worthy to be worshiped.

God is sovereign. He knows the end result of all things from the very beginning with perfect unimaginable reason, detail, and clarity. He has a purpose for everything even though we may not see it nor understand all of life's events as they unfold. Whether anyone agrees or disagrees is completely irrelevant.

God is omnipotent. He is all-powerful beyond anything anyone can imagine. There is nothing God cannot do. His infinite energy cannot ever be depleted in any way. He directs traffic in every atom in existence throughout the vast immeasurable universe with unfathomable precision.

God is omniscient. He knows all things from the infinitesimally minute to the largest gargantuan bodies known and unknown to man floating around in space. He is never surprised by anything that takes place anywhere. There cannot possibly be any discovery by human beings nor anyone else, that God was not previously aware of.

God is omnipresent. He is always everywhere. Nothing can ever be hidden from Him.

God is just. He is the only righteous one and He rules with absolute perfect justice in all instances. He hates sin in ways we humans cannot even imagine. All sin in any amount and in any form is an offence to His being and it must be dealt with in a perfectly just way.

God is the source of goodness and mercy. The oxygen in the air, the warmth provided by the sun, the water, the food grown on earth, along with the natural resources all belong to God.

Everyone, believers and non-believers alike benefit from God's design of our planet.

God is love. His Son, Jesus who was without sin, suffered and died in our place to pay the full price for our sins against Him. This was done in order that those of us who believe may be in God's presence after we die.

God never needs any counseling of any kind nor for any reason. He designed the earth and everything else in perfect balance. Known as the science of isostasy, He weighed the land masses, the mountains and the oceans with indescribable precision in order that the earth rotates and moves perfectly through space as if held by nothing. We have knowledge that we are constantly rotating and moving at great speeds while standing still on the earth's surface, but we feel only a breeze. Everything is being sustained inexplicably and seemingly without effort by none other than God Himself.

Fear not, for I am with you; Be not dismayed, for I am your God. I will strengthen you, yes, I will help you, I will uphold you with My righteous right hand. (Isaiah 41:10)

Biblical Truth from Chapter #2

God exists and He is in full control over His entire creation from beginning to end.

What do you personally think because it matters? Can you possibly try to wrap your mind around who God is? Have you taken the time to investigate for yourself? Are you willing to write it down and put your name on it?

I challenge you to do your own research and then think for yourself. In order to believe the future things to come, you must first believe that God is real and that He is an eternal supernatural being. God alone is trustworthy. God alone is worthy to be worshiped. We must be humble enough to accept the fact that He surpasses all human understanding. There is nothing more comforting than having the assurance of being spared from the devastation of the future things to come.

CHAPTER 3

Heaven & Hell

It is said by many that Sir Isaac Newton (1643 - 1727) had no equals in the history of science. He was an English mathematician and among the greatest scientific geniuses of all times. Newton was also an astronomer, a physicist, a theologian, and an author. He discovered the law of gravitation, formulated the basic laws of motion, developed calculus, and analyzed the nature of white light.

Behind all his scientific work and discoveries, Newton was convinced that God had made the universe with a precise mathematical structure. At the same time, he also concluded that God had gifted man's mind to understand that structure. It's as if God wanted us to get to know Him a bit better. The precise order and design of the universe spoke volumes about God's awesome majesty and wisdom.

Newton concluded that apart from God, nothing could have come into existence. He also understood that the greatness and power of God is beyond any human comprehension. One of his greatest quotes goes something like this:

I must confess to a feeling of profound humility in the presence of a universe which transcends us at almost every point. I feel like a child who while playing by the seashore has found a few bright colored shells and a few pebbles while the whole vast ocean of truth stretches out almost untouched and unruffled before my eager fingers.

So, if we've come to accept the truth of God's existence, His creation and His supernatural means of sustaining it, then it's reasonable to also believe the biblical claim regarding a real place called heaven and a real place called hell. Simply stated, heaven is the place where the eternal souls of believers in God end up after they die. The opposite end of the spectrum is that hell is the place where the eternal souls of non-believers in God end up after they die. Heaven is freedom and eternal bliss. Hell is bondage and eternal pain.

Before we get to the future things to come, it's important to understand the main and most important message of the entire Bible from start to finish. It is one of *redemption*. We're all part of this entire story throughout human history since time first began with the creation of Adam and Eve. Now, in order for something or someone to be redeemed, there must be something wrong. The problem is sin, and we are all guilty of it regardless of the degree of sin. God's message throughout His Word, the Bible, is that He provided a way to redeem us so that we do not have to suffer the penalty of sin. He designed a way for us to end up in heaven and thus in His presence.

> *For all have sinned and fall short of the glory of God.* (Romans 3:23)

> *For the wages of sin is death, but the gift of God is eternal life in Christ Jesus our Lord.* (Romans 6:23)

Since the very beginning of creation, the first two people on earth, Adam and Eve, sinned by not having kept God's command to not eat the fruit from the tree of knowledge of good and evil (Genesis 2:16-17). The penalty for this disobedience is described in Genesis chapter 3 and is known as *the fall of man*. As a result, all of humanity is born with an inherent fallen nature. We are all prone to sin. In fact, the entire universe was cursed by God from that point forward to this very day.

It is this fallen sinful nature of mankind that requires redemption in order for anyone to end up in God's presence, as He is the only one who is holy and perfectly just. We live in a fallen world where there is death, disease, suffering, and all kinds of unspeakable sins being committed daily. You might not think you're part of the problem but just have a look at Romans 3:23 again and recognize that these are God's words. Without the one and only holy Redeemer, God's only Son Jesus, there is no hope for anyone ending up in heaven.

So, with the above as a very brief background, it's safe to say that heaven is the goal, for most people I would assume.

Knowing for sure that you were one of the redeemed would likely make your day. Heaven is the happy forever-after place we want to end up in. It is the desired outcome as the final destination for the eternal souls of people. It is where we will experience perfect peace forever.

If someone were to walk up to you and say something like *there is a place called heaven where there are streets made of gold. Do you think you will end up there after you die?* Would you dismiss this question? Do you think heaven is some kind of fantasy land, or would you be curious enough to want to know more about it because you may not be sure? I would also venture to guess that most people would respond with *yes, I think or at least I hope that I will end up there because a good God will probably let me in.*

Before we have a closer look into this, I wanted to point out that I mentioned earlier that *most people* regarded heaven as the goal destination for their eternal soul. It should come as no surprise that there are some people who simply dismiss any possibility of an afterlife. This group of atheists believe that there is nothing after life on earth ends. They go about their daily routines not really considering where we came from, and much less about the one of two places where souls will end up afterwards.

Lastly, as difficult as it may be to believe, there are also some folks who want nothing to do with heaven. They proudly and loudly declare that they would rather end up in hell. This third group seems to think that it would be more exciting somehow to worship Satan who is God's main adversary. They might even think there's a big party down there and they don't seem to want to miss out.

By way of a brief biblical review, Satan was once Lucifer, God's highest angelic creation. Because of prideful rebellion and self-exaltation, Lucifer was cast out of heaven along with some of the other angels who followed Lucifer as they also rebelled against God. Ever since then, the main agenda for Satan and the fallen demonic angels was to thwart God's plan for the salvation and redemption of human souls through any means and at every turn.

It has to be stated in plain terms that Satan is no match for God in any way whatsoever. However, Satan can easily overpower and overwhelm anyone who does not have God on his or her side. We should always be on guard and not underestimate nor overestimate Satan's influence as he goes about his work of deception and destruction.

Among other titles, Satan is also known as the following:

- Prince of this World (John 12:31)
- Enemy (Matthew 13:25)
- Prince of the Power of the Air (Ephesians 2:2)
- The Wicked One (Ephesians 6:16)
- Father of Lies (John 8:44)
- Murderer (John 8:44)
- Prince of Demons (Matthew 12:24-26)
- Deceiver of the Whole Word (Revelation 12:9)

Through the use of all sorts of schemes, lies and deceptions of the highest order, Satan is a master at using seemingly innocent temptations which end up exploding into horrible addictions with bad endings. He and his followers are constantly roaming around the entire globe constantly introducing doubt, chaos and confusion. Across all nations and for all people everywhere, Satan's intention is to disrupt every facet of people's lives. Sadly, it's working.

> *Be sober, be vigilant; because your adversary the devil walks about like a roaring lion, seeking whom he may devour.* (1 Peter 5:8).

Satan wants nothing more than for as many unsuspecting souls as possible to end up in hell. Although he can roam freely on earth now, he knows that hell will be his final destination. He is always on the lookout to seduce people from across the globe to join him there. He is the source of all evil everywhere. Once in hell, the grim and hopeless reality will surely sink in.

- Darkness
- Torment
- Weeping
- Wailing
- Gnashing of teeth
- Guilt
- Regret
- Continuous pain and punishment with no relief
- Eternal lake of fire

For those ending up down there, this unimaginable living hell will have only just begun for all eternity. There will be no escape from this place. There will be no appeals entertained.

There will be no more chances for a re-do. Complete and perfect justice will have been finalized. There will certainly be no party.

As expected, heaven will be the exact opposite of hell. The reality of these two end destinations existing and waiting for people's eternal bodies and souls is no different than the reality of me writing these words and you reading them at this very moment. As you continue to move forward, I will continue to say *just think for yourself* as there is nothing more important to you personally than where you end up.

To try and get an idea of what heaven will be like, we need to once again turn to the biblical text. It's what God revealed to us as He wanted us to know and not remain ignorant. I will first say that any words used to describe heaven will be limited at best and will fall way short of its actual splendor and majesty. After all, it is the place where God, the Creator of the universe, dwells.

I have often said that the word *awesome* should be strictly reserved for use in a sentence or phrase when describing God or heaven. I just get the sense that anyone who has the privilege of being in heaven and in God's presence, will simply be in a state of complete and total awe. We will be speechless with never-ending opportunities to explore, worship and learn about an infinite, awesome God. The following are but a few points regarding heaven:

- ▷ A place where there are only those who know, love and serve the Lord Jesus, the one and only true Redeemer.
- ▷ A place where there are no seas. (Revelation 21:1)

- A place with no sorrow, no tears, no pain and no death. (Revelation 21:4)
- A place where there is no need for a sun there because God's glory will shine permanently. (Revelation 21:23)
- A place with no more curse as there is no more sin. (Revelation 22:3)
- A place with no night and therefore no fear nor anxiety of any sort. (Revelation 22:5)
- A place where the New Jerusalem will be the great heavenly city of perfect holiness.
- A place of indescribable beautiful lights shining from and throughout the magnificent city from God's glory like a clear, translucent diamond.
- A great wall around the city measures about 72 yards thick and 1,380 miles high on each of the four equal sides same as its height making it as the shape of a cube. (Revelation 21:16-17)
- A total of 12 massive gates (three on each side) for each of the 12 tribes of Israel. Each gate is made of a single pearl spanning a height of 1,400 miles high providing access to the city from all directions. (Revelation 21:21)
- The street of the heavenly city is pure translucent gold.
- A place of splendor, beauty, magnificence, holiness, absolute purity, with an eternal life-giving river clear as crystal whose source is the Lord Jesus Himself.
- A place of absolute absence of any sort of physical or spiritual disease.

The purpose of this chapter was to provide only a small window for us to peek into what is revealed in God's Word regarding heaven and hell. This only scratches the surface although there has been lots of ink spilled in many books on the subject throughout history. This was important to consider and understand as we continue moving forward toward identifying the future things to come.

Biblical Truth from Chapter #3

Believers will end up in heaven while non-believers will end up in hell for eternity.

What do you personally think because it matters? Do you believe there is a real heaven and a real hell where our souls end up after we die? Have you talked with anyone who knows more than you about the subject? Are you willing to write it down and put your name on it?

Whether or not you believe heaven and hell exist, certainly matters but the truth is that it's irrelevant. Just in case you were wondering where I stand on this subject, I do not doubt their existence. Being sure of heaven as your final destination is more comforting than you can imagine. You will have the assurance of being spared from the devastation of the future things to come.

CHAPTER 4

Chosen to Believe

It's a common expression as I'm sure most people would agree. *Everything happens for a reason.* In case I had not mentioned it yet, I continue to believe that there is a very good reason you're reading this little book right now. It may be that you were thinking of the bigger picture in life and wondered how you fit into it or how it all ends. It may be that a friend of yours gave you this book or someone may have suggested it. Or, it may have been divine intervention and it was meant for you to be exactly where you are, regardless of how you arrived at this point.

Perhaps you are already a believer in God, creation, redemption, and all the future things to come. If that is the case, then perhaps this will serve as reassurance and comfort to you. Perhaps there is someone in your life who you can now encourage to seek God as well because they were meant to believe also. Regardless, it may be a sign for you to pay it forward to show that you care enough to share the good news with someone else.

> *From everyone to whom much is given, from him much will be required* (Luke 12:48).

I have been blessed beyond description throughout my life and I am truly humbled as I am writing this. Yes, I want to add value and no, I don't want to waste anybody's time. I am also not naïve enough to think that I need to drag someone into reading about a subject which I believe to be important, that they would then somehow agree with me much less see what I see.

No pictures, no words, no books, no history lessons, nor banging on drums to cause attention will ever be enough to cause everyone to believe. It was meant to be this way from the very beginning. It has simply been on my heart to want to share God's biblical message and His amazing grace toward me on these few pages. I feel this within my being from a sense of joyful responsibility as well as an honorable duty to fulfill by faith, all for God's glory.

The main message of this chapter, *Chosen to Believe*, may not be as familiar nor as popular, but this does not make it less relevant. Admittedly, it's a concept not readily understood. It may simply not resonate with all individuals in the same way, even though it is biblical and thus true. Unfortunately, it will likely not resonate with most. If you have never heard of it before, I would venture to guess that your first reaction would be that it's not fair somehow. However, if you feel compelled in the slightest and you hear that inner voice which causes you enough to be curious, then I would encourage you to keep reading further.

> *You did not choose Me, but I chose you and appointed you that you should go and bear fruit, and that your fruit should remain, that whatever you ask the Father in My name He may give you.* (John 15:16)

> *Moreover, whom He predestined, these He also called; whom He called, these He also justified; and whom He justified, these He also glorified.* (Romans 8:29)

> *Just as He chose us in Him before the foundations of the world, that we should be holy and without blame before Him in love having predestined us to adoption as sons by Jesus Christ to Himself, according to the good pleasure of His will.* (Ephesians 1:4-5)

The main message of this chapter is that all individuals whoever walked the earth *and believed* in God, creation, and His plan for redemption were *chosen to believe* by God Himself before He even created the universe. Just try and let that sink in for a minute. Only those individuals who were meant to believe were chosen as God's own elect from before the very first day in existence.

Before all of creation, before the very beginning of time, God in His infinite wisdom and sovereignty chose those individuals who would end up believing. As evidence has clearly shown throughout history, not everyone who was ever born believed because those individuals were simply not part of the chosen ones. Only those who were predestined to believe were handpicked by the one and only true God, not only by Himself but also for Himself and to the praise of His own glory.

The doctrine of election is emphasized many times throughout the Bible although I have only listed three verses above. Regardless of anyone's opinion or how you may personally feel about this, redemption of those who were chosen to believe since before the beginning of time continues to this very day. It is also worth noting that God alone is the one who granted the faith needed for those who were chosen to end up believing. No person who believes could ever brag about anything they may have said or done, as salvation from sin cannot be earned in any way by anyone.

> *For by grace you have been saved through faith, and that not of yourselves; it is the gift of God, not of works, lest anyone should boast.* (Ephesians 2:8-9)

This process will continue until all the predestined believers yet to be born will have been redeemed. After the very last one from God's sovereign design is brought into the fold of believers, then the subsequent phases of the future things to come will begin to manifest themselves for everyone to see.

Until then, we move forward in faith knowing that God is in full control of all events. Nobody except God the Father knows who the last chosen believer will be and exactly when that person will end up believing.

What I also know for sure is that I do not deserve to have been chosen to believe but I'm glad that I was on the list. The older I get, the less worthy I truly feel, having been blessed with God's mercy. I'm grateful beyond words that God granted me enough faith to believe. I have done nothing to deserve any of it. It is by His grace alone that I am here today writing this. He drew me closer and helped me want to learn more about who He is. Apart from God's overwhelming grace, I honestly don't think that any of us who believe know precisely why we were initially chosen to believe. I also have no doubt that we are all glad that He did.

Given the opportunity of letting others know about God's amazing love, I know that all believers are all willing to spread the word. It's the very least we could do as we point others toward Him and Jesus, the one and only Redeemer. Those of us who believe were chosen by God in eternity past and were called according to His sovereign purpose. Those whom God elected, and Christ has died for will be saved.

This biblical doctrine of having been chosen to believe may seem a bit overwhelming at first. I mean, why some people and not others? I remember that it took me a while to wrap my mind around God having known me before He created heaven and earth. God knows of everyone who was ever born including those yet to be born. This includes those who would end up believing as well as those who would end up not believing. By faith, I know that I was meant to be born at a specific time in history, I was meant to believe, and I was meant to share my story with you at this moment. As to why, I will continue to trust that God knows better and hope that you're on the list too.

So, how can you be sure if you were chosen to believe? You will feel the tugging on your heart strings as well as a feeling that something is not quite right in your life. When looking in the mirror and honestly pondering about whether you will end up in heaven, you will simply not be sure. You will have some increased anxiety about this as time marches forward. Your human pride will kick into overdrive trying to pull you back into a state of confusion. Your tendencies will be to avoid it because you can't make much sense of it. Your internal struggle will continue until you consider that there may be something beyond your understanding. You will conclude that it's possible you may need some sort of help beyond any human intervention, so it may be worth pursuing. You will not be able to resist God's calling.

You will be drawn into learning more about the one and only true and perfectly holy triune God, His nature and His grand design for all of creation. You will want to seek biblical doctrine as it is the source for God's revelation to us human beings for our own good. You will want to learn more about His laws and ordinances, and you will begin to move in His direction. Your level of understanding will increase to the point where you will know in your heart that you are totally depraved and hopeless without a redeemer.

You will come to realize how your sinful nature is an offense to a holy God beyond description and the price for this penalty will need to be paid. You will know beyond the shadow of a doubt that you will need God's forgiveness in order to end up in His presence one day. You will be grateful beyond words, and you will believe that God's son, Jesus had already paid the price in full on your behalf.

You will be forgiven, and you will know for sure that you will end up in heaven after you die. You will turn a new page in your life as if born again, you will recognize, and you will gladly and willingly turn away from your previous sinful ways. You will want to increase your relationship with the One who redeemed you. You will want to talk with and hang out with other believers. You will want to share your story with non-believers. You will sleep well every night knowing for sure that you were chosen to believe. The scary devastating events of the future things to come will no longer weigh on your mind.

Biblical Truth from Chapter #4

Before creation, God alone has chosen some people to believe and be saved.

What do you personally think because it matters? If you find yourself merely wondering whether you were also chosen to believe, even if you're not sure at this point, then you're on the right track. Pay attention to that inner voice and keep seeking the truth from God Himself who is the source of all truth. Talk with other believers openly and honestly. With patience, humility, and an open heart, continue to ask for God's help, guidance, instruction and mercy until you know for sure.

I know that God created the entire universe, and I also know that He can certainly help you as well. Will you consider God's gift of salvation? Are you willing to write it down and commit pursuing Him? There is nothing more comforting than having the assurance of being spared from the devastation of the future things to come.

CHAPTER 5

Relationships

Celebrations are not only fun but they are also important to people everywhere. They're part of the human fabric. Birthdays, weddings, graduations, a new exiting job and even retirement are all reasons for us to get together. There are also the yearly holidays like Memorial Day, Independence Day, Thanksgiving, and Christmas, among others. These are all opportunities for us to gather and enjoy our time with family and friends sharing and strengthening our relationships.

When I was growing up as a teenager, I tried out and joined a local travel soccer league that included some of the best players from the area where we lived. I had started playing much earlier as a kid and I loved to play every chance I got. There were several teams in the city and ours was sponsored by a little store which sold trophies.

I remember the guys on our team thought it was cool to have a trophy logo on our soccer jerseys while dreaming of getting the real one if we won the season. Back in those days, only the winning team players got a trophy. The runner up team may have received a small cheap medal of some sort. You likely figured out that there were no participation trophies handed out to all teams in the league. Some may even say *those were the good old days.*

We had a very intense coach who was married with a young family, but he knew the game very well. We didn't always like our coach's practices because all the drills were exhausting. He took the game quite seriously, but he also had fun and knew how to focus on each player. Our coach took the time to help us improve individually and also playing as a team. He got to know us not only as players but also as individuals with strengths and weaknesses. He was always coming up with drills and challenging us to get better with a focus toward achieving a common goal. He was one of the best soccer coaches I have ever played for.

As the season started, we noticed that the league was full of excellent teams. Every game was all about getting to the final to get a shot at that trophy. After only a few losses, we won most other key games and made it to the final one. This was the game we looked forward to all season. All the bleachers were full, and we were playing under the big lights on a beautiful late summer night sky. Our coach seemed a bit nervous, but we all knew we were prepared and ready to go.

The game went back and forth but ended in a 3-3 tie. After two exciting overtime periods the game was still tied, now at

5-5. We now needed a shootout where each team were to take five penalty shots in order to decide the winner. Our sharpshooters scored at every one of our turns while our opponents missed the net a couple of times and our goalie made a save. We had just won the biggest game of our young lives. We looked over at the sidelines, and our coach was jumping and running around as if he was the one who just won the world cup. He was totally ecstatic. We had just won the city championship and we were all incredibly happy. We each got a trophy.

Our coach wanted the entire team to celebrate together with his family, so he invited all the players at his house one afternoon the following week for a barbeque. After all, we had a particularly good reason to celebrate. We were a team and we cared about each other. We practiced hard, we played together, we stood up for one another and we invested time getting to know each other. We had built a bond and there was a relationship between us players as well as our coach.

I didn't bring up this story to brag about a championship soccer team I was fortunate to be a part of during my youth. I have no doubt you may have similar stories. Perhaps you also became close to team members, or coaches, or colleagues, or siblings, or cousins, or even parents. Maybe you shared memorable adventures with friends and over time you became close. I brought up the soccer story to make a point about something we're all aware of. Relationships are priceless. It's all about those you care about, and those you check in with if only on occasion, and those you spend time with, and those who you turn to for help, and those who you will also lend a helping hand.

I mentioned at the beginning of this chapter that we relish

the time when we get together and celebrate various occasions. It's obvious that we get together with those we know. We care about their wellbeing, and we will pitch in when someone we know needs help. It's how it was meant to be. To the best of our abilities, we will be there to laugh and celebrate together. We will also be there to offer support, share memories, mourn and even cry together at funerals. A rich and fulfilled life is about sharing it with those we have a relationship with.

Every one of us often invite those in our lives over to our place for a special occasion or sometimes for no reason at all other than just to catch up. We in turn find ourselves being invited to their place on occasion as well for similar reasons. Furthermore, if someone we knew showed up unexpectedly, we would just ask them inside to see what was up, as they might need help. It's just how relationships work.

What if you were to consider any of the following people in the list below? Assuming there is no relationship with any of them, would you just invite them to your place for any reason? Also, would you expect an invitation from them anytime soon? Better yet, if you just showed up at their doorstep one day, would you expect that they let you in?

- The mayor of the city you live in.
- The CEO of the largest company in your state.
- The most sought-after movie star in Hollywood.
- The most popular music artist.
- The highest paid athlete in the world.
- The president or prime minister of the country you live in.

- ▷ The Queen of England.
- ▷ Any Royal Monarch on planet earth.
- ▷ Anyone of the highest stature you can think of so, fill in the blank __.

Unless you personally know any of these people on the list above and they also know you, it's safe to say that you are all strangers to each other. You would not invite them over to your house because you don't know them. Likewise, they would not send out an invitation for you to come by and visit with them because they don't know you. And, if you were to just show up at their doorstep, or their gate, or their palace, let's just take the leap and say that there is a very good chance that they would also not let you in. That's just how it is.

What about God, the Creator of the universe? He already knows who you are because there is nothing He does not know. The question is *do you know Him?* Notice the question is not do you know *of Him*, because you may know *of* all the people on the list above as well. The real question is *do you really know God, and do you have a relationship with Him?* More importantly, if you were to show up at the gates of heaven where God dwells, *do you think He will let you in?*

The mere contemplation for the difference between any of the people on the list above and God Himself, one would find it to be a mind-numbing immeasurable chasm. There is obviously no comparison between God and anyone else anywhere. Some people may think that those shown on the list above are noteworthy, and that may be the case to some limited extent here on earth. The fact remains that none of them would let you into their house because you have no relationship with them. It boggles the mind that some folks have the foolish audacity to think that if they had no relationship with God while they were alive, and then showed up at the gates of heaven after they die, they would be allowed inside anyway.

Did I also mention that for any relationship with other people as well as with God to be meaningful, it needs to be genuine? We all know people in our lives perhaps acquaintances, friends, or even family members, who seem to be on guard whenever a get together takes place. They seem to prefer to live in the shadows somehow, seem disingenuous at best, not even inquiring about your wellbeing, if only on occasion. They pop up from time to time and you're just not sure if you're witnessing a façade of some sort. Some of these relationships are superficial at best without any real substance beneath the surface.

Having a genuine meaningful relationship with someone is not about airing dirty laundry nor about gossip. It's simply about honestly trying to get to know each other, to share experiences in your lives, and to help each other because you care. It's about integrity, mutual respect, and appreciation for each other. I recognize we all have personal concerns and private matters we deal with individually. However, being genuine in any worthwhile relationship is a prerequisite and it's a two-way street. Once again, that's just how it is.

Yes, we are all flawed but I've said for a long time that character matters, and a person's true colors will eventually shine bright for all to see. What appears to be hidden deep inside each of us will eventually surface as interactions take place with the passage of time. People may end up fooling other people for a little while but trying to fool God is simply futile.

> *Not everyone who says to Me, "Lord, Lord," shall enter the kingdom of heaven, but he who does the will of My Father in heaven.* (Matthew 7:21)

> *Many will say to Me in that day, "Lord, Lord, have we not prophesied in Your name, cast out demons in Your name?"* (Matthew 7:22)

> *And then I will declare to them, "I never knew you; depart from Me, you who practice lawlessness!"* (Matthew 7:23)

Nobody can *buy* their way into heaven. Nobody can *be good enough* to get into heaven on their own merits. Nobody can *do* enough of anything to gain God's favor to allow them into heaven. Nobody can fool God into thinking they're something they're obviously not. Not even those who think they are *holier than thou* who have said or done things just so they can boast about it to other people. God alone knows the heart and He alone knows everyone's intentions when it comes to a genuine relationship with Him. Pretending is foolish and just not worth anything.

A proper relationship takes time, and it requires honesty and humility on your part. God wants you to get to know Him personally. He already knows who you are, He knows where you're from, and He knows what you've done. Despite all of that, He still wants to have a relationship with you, but it has to be a two-way genuine one. Why would anyone foolishly think that God would allow them to spend eternity in heaven with Him after trying their best to avoid Him and flat out insult Him while here on earth? I've heard of this being referred to as totally absurd and to me, that sounds more than reasonable.

I mentioned earlier that to the best of my ability, I would be respectfully straight up and not sugarcoat things. I will always challenge and encourage you to do your own research as well as for you to think for yourself. Whether you have a genuine relationship with the One and only true Triune God is a relevant point for you to evaluate seriously while you can. Whether anyone agrees if that's a fair standard is completely irrelevant, even if you were to debate the subject. This real relationship with God is something that is personal, totally applicable to each of us individually, and necessary for access to heaven. You will be glad beyond words during this life on earth and afterwards.

Biblical Truth from Chapter #5

Having a genuine personal relationship with God is a prerequisite to ending up in heaven.

What do you personally think because it matters? Are you at all concerned about your current relationship with the Creator of the universe? Do you want to get to know Him better? If so, are you willing to write it down and put your name on it?

Every single person who believes, will have a genuine relationship with God. That's how we know for sure that we will end up in heaven. It was designed this way from the very beginning for our own good. There is nothing more comforting than having the assurance of being spared from the devastation of the future things to come.

_____

_____

_____

_____

_____

_____

_____

CHAPTER 6

ALL PUFFED-UP

On November 22, 1963, then US president John F. Kennedy was scheduled to deliver some remarks at the Trade Mart in Dallas, Texas later that day. Before he had a chance to arrive there, the whole world watched in horror as he was assassinated while on route, and the speech remained undelivered. Although worth reading it in its entirety, the following paragraph was written at the end of the speech:

We in this country, in this generation, are – by destiny rather than choice – the watchmen on the walls of world freedom. We ask, therefore, that we may be worthy of our power and responsibility, that we may exercise our strength with wisdom and restraint, and that we may achieve in our time and for all time the ancient vision of "peace on earth, good will toward men." That must always be our goal, and the righteousness of our cause must always underlie our strength. For as was written long ago: "except the Lord keep the city, the watchman waketh but in vain."

President John F. Kennedy went down in history as a beloved president. The last sentence from that paragraph above came from Psalm 127 originating during biblical times by King Solomon.

> *Unless the Lord builds the house, they labor in vain who built it; Unless the Lord guards the city, the watchman stays awake in vain.* (Psalm 127:1)

The United States of America has been an extraordinary superpower in the world for a long time. I also find it no coincidence that the US has been blessed over the decades and centuries. After all, the US motto is *In God We Trust*, and that phrase is even written on the US currency as well within the House Chamber of the US Congress.

Former president Ronald Reagan once said, *America is a shining city upon a hill whose beacon light guides freedom-loving people everywhere.* Despite its shortcomings, people from across the globe are still striving to arrive here in the US to this day. People in general, want to escape all kinds of problems, war, oppression and tyranny. The country is still looked at as offering hope and opportunity for a better life for many across the globe. I am fortunate and appreciative beyond words for having experienced the legal immigration process firsthand, as well as becoming a US citizen. It is a privilege and I do not take it for granted. The brave men and women who have fought for the freedoms we all enjoy here in the US are second to none and I thank God for them.

Other countries have taken note of both the good and bad aspects of the freedoms we have enjoyed in the US. Arguably, ill-intended individuals across the globe as well as within the US continue to look for ways to disrupt any sense of normalcy. This is only to say that the forces of good and evil have been hard at work everywhere for centuries. This should come as no surprise to any God-fearing believer.

However, over the course of time, we as people from all over the globe have gradually but deliberately moved away from the divine Creator of the universe. The houses we build are no longer built with a desire for His protection as Psalm 127:1 has warned us about. The watchmen of the cities stay awake in vain if the Lord God is not wanted there.

There have been attempts, some successful, to remove God from our society at large. Is it too late for people across the world to return to God's ways? Perhaps no, it's not too late, but given the evidence, I would argue that these are all obvious signs of the end times within God's grand design for humanity. We all have front row seats to the world events, so hang on tight as you continue reading through the chapters ahead.

From ancient times, kings, monarchs, leaders and powerful people displayed their wealth by building tall and magnificent structures. The Egyptians built pyramids to show off how rich they were. All people from all ages want to show prestige and recognition for their accomplishments.

How high could we build? Just have a look at how far we've come as well as the bizarre concepts proposed for the not-too-distant future. The list below is shown in order of structure height from shortest to tallest so it's worth noting the heights shown in meters (kilometers). You may recognize some existing buildings across the world, some may be news to you, while others are planned to be built as indicated by the year in parenthesis.

- Eifel Tower (1889) – Paris, France – 324 m
- Empire State Building (1931) – New York, USA – 443 m
- Shanghai World Financial Center (2007) – Shanghai, China – 474 m
- Taipei 101 (2004) – Taiwan – 509 m
- Guangzhou CTF Finance Center (2016) - Guangzhou, China – 530 m
- One World Trade Center (2014) – New York, USA – 541 m
- Lotte World Tower (2017) – Seoul, South Korea - 556 m
- Ping An Finance Center (2017) - Shenzhen, China – 599 m
- Abraj Al-Bait Clock Tower (2012) - Mecca, Saudi Arabia – 601 m
- Shanghai Tower (2015) - Shanghai, China – 632 m
- Merdeka PNB 118 (Est. 2022) – Kuala Lumpur, Malaysia - 644 m
- **Burj Khalifa (2010) – Dubai, UAE – Currently tallest in the world – 828 m**
- Jeddah Tower (Construction halted in 2017) – Saudi Arabia – Planned for 1,000+ m
- Burj Mubarak al-Kabir (Estimated 2023 to 2030) – Kuwait – Planned for 1,001 m
- Dubai Creek Tower (Construction halted in 2018. Estimated 2022) – Dubai, UAE – 1,350 m

- ▷ Sky Mile Tower (Concept only. Estimated 2045) – Tokyo, Japan – 1,700 m (1.7 km.)
- ▷ Times Square 3015 (Concept only. Estimated 2050) – New York, USA – 1,733 m (1.73 km.)
- ▷ X-Seed 4000 (Concept only) - Tokyo, Japan – 4,000 m (4 km) – To house 1 million people
- ▷ Tokyo Tower of Babel (Concept only) – Tokyo, Japan – 10,000 m (10 km.) - Taller than Mt. Everest, this would be tallest object on planet earth – To house 30 million people – Estimated time for completion is 150 years.
- ▷ The Launch Loop (Concept only) – "The sky isn't the limit" – 80,000 m (80 km.) – To propel objects into space through a magnetic levitation system at speeds up to 14 km./sec.
- ▷ Space Elevator (Concept only) – An elevator into space – 35,800,000 m (35,800 km.) – If approved, Japan claims estimated completion by 2050. China estimates completion by 2045.

The current tallest building in the world is the Burj Khalifa located in Dubai, UAE and its height is 828 meters. It's a magnificent structure and it's *just barely over one-half mile high*. Now, can you imagine buildings *twice the height* of the Burj Khalifa? That building would be over a mile high in the air where it is proposed the population of an entire city of 1 million people could dwell in it.

What about behemoth structures higher than Mt. Everest approaching *six miles in the air* with footprints double the area of Dallas, Texas proposed to house about 30 million people?

That is just under the entire population of Canada. How about this space elevator reaching outer space to 22,245 miles above the earth? How does this thing hang onto the earth as it rotates about its axis? Who would you call if the elevator got stuck halfway up? Wow!!!

The idea of reaching to the sky is not new and I'm not oblivious to the benefits of skyscrapers. Human innovation is truly remarkable, but can we all agree that there is a limit? Reading about some of these concepts leads me to believe that our human pride is not only flying high but that it's out of control. We think we're all that, and countries across the globe are racing to show off in ways that defy common sense. There is even an imaginary real estate market now. Money is no object, and the sky is the limit. We choose to ignore God's presence in our lives and our pride get us *all puffed-up.*

> *By pride comes nothing but strife, but with the well-advised is wisdom.* (Proverbs 13:10)
>
> *He who is of a proud heart stirs up strife, but he who trusts in the Lord will be prospered.* (Proverbs 28:25)
>
> *Do not be puffed-up with pride. Tremble rather, for if God did not spare the natural branches, neither will He spare you.* (Romans 11:21)

The evidence is everywhere. More and more people think that they can continue to exist indefinitely on this remarkable planet earth without any intervention from God Himself. They simply refuse to believe He exists much less that He created the entire universe, and He presently sustains it. They are deliberately walking away from His original design and protection. Can the division of various opinions among many people in the world today be any greater than it happens to be at this very moment? The sad truth is that yes, of course it can.

Considering the general unrest and the fragile world events taking place, it certainly feels like the final countdown toward the end times is getting closer. Humanity appears to be setting the stage for its own extinction, given the massive weapons the superpowers of the world possess. Huge buildings and structures with unrealistic projections, family principles being eroded, intolerance to varying opinions, neighbor against neighbor, kids against parents, cyberattacks, space wars, socio-economic-political-racial divide, left-right extremes, etcetera, are all right in our face daily.

Pride and arrogance have caused the downfall of every powerful nation throughout history. These are among the best in Satan's arsenal toward achieving godlessness and they are obviously working. Because of blatant disobedience and idolatry, unsuspecting folks as well as entire nations have steadily removed themselves away from God's ways and His protection. From His original elect, Israel, to Assyria, to Babylon, to Medo-Persia, to Greece, to the Roman empire, to the current superpowers in the world today, the writing is on the wall. In the end, God is going to win exactly as written in His Word, the Bible.

The more time passes, the farther away from God humanity seems to drift. We begin to believe that we can become totally independent of Him, and we even start entertaining the idea that we can live on Mars, probably to get away from Him. As the expression goes, *the longer you're in a rut, the deeper you sink*. We stubbornly refuse to acknowledge we're in trouble as a society, and don't ask for God's help. The longer we commit an offense, the more resistant and blinder to the truth we become. The longer an estranged relationship festers, the closer we get to the point of no return.

Biblical Truth from Chapter #6

Being all puffed-up with pride and arrogance will lead to your eternal destruction.

What do you personally think because it matters? How do you interpret current world events? Is the world at large getting closer or farther away from God? What is your opinion on this subject? Are you willing to write it down and put your name on it?

The entire world is connected in more ways than ever before, and it seems to be moving toward a sort of universal conformity, away from biblical doctrine. More importantly, are you prepared by having God's protection going forward? There is nothing more comforting than having the assurance of being spared from the devastation of the future things to come.

CHAPTER 7

DEBT + DOUBT = DEATH

Throughout history, evil forces have meandered among many people to corrupt them as well as governments across the globe. As a reminder, the most basic main purpose of any government is to protect the life and property of its citizens. Without question, despicable atrocities have been well documented where some governments took devastating actions against not only other nations, but also against the people of their own country. Sadly, the likelihood is high that countless other evil acts remain covered up to this day.

Because Satan is very crafty, he uses deception and introduces doubt at every opportunity possible. It's the method he used to cause Adam and Eve to doubt God Himself in the Garden of Eden. He wants to cause confusion and chaos among the masses. He seduces people and governments alike across the land with the sole purpose of setting them up for their ultimate destruction.

These dark forces continue lurking about, creating the illusion that things are under control when in fact that is far from the truth. Crime, extortion, bribery, sex trafficking, self-serving laws, and all sorts of other sins and illegal activities sneak up and create massive problems over time. The problems may manifest themselves at the beginning as relatively small, but they eventually surface with a vengeance spreading exponentially like a deadly cancer against humanity at large.

One such giant problem is debt. Would you consider it to be a problem in the world today? I'm not referring to the kind of debt that someone might have in the form of a mortgage-type debt for a house. I'm talking about the kind of debt that keeps rising without the hope of ever paying it back. The kind of debt that is out of control, where checks and balances are absent or not enforced at all. The kind of debt that appears to involve smoke and mirrors because it's unmanageable. The kind of debt where there appears to be no accountability in sight and hardly anyone is paying attention to.

According to the World Debt Clock, the list below shows the **National Debt** of some developed countries shown in US dollars. These figures shown are as of mid-May 2021 and for emphasis are ***trillions of US dollars*** rounded to the nearest decimal point.

- USA . . . . $28.3 Trillion
- Japan . . . . $14.8 Trillion
- China . . . . $8.1 Trillion

- ▷ United Kingdom .... $3.6 Trillion
- ▷ France .... $3.2 Trillion
- ▷ India .... $2.6 Trillion
- ▷ Canada .... $1.9 Trillion

Essentially, the debt of these nations is the amount of money each country has spent over and above the amount they receive in revenue from taxes and other such forms of income. In other words, a simplified formula can be expressed as **National Expenses – National Income = National Debt.** These debts continue to increase every single second of every hour of every day.

Every country continues to spend more money than they receive in tax revenues. Every year, their national debt levels have increased to where they are today and counting. Just try and let these numbers sink in for a minute. The USA is currently the most indebted nation on earth. Do you think this debt could ever be paid back? Oh, and in case you're wondering who this debt is owed to, or who keeps lending them the money in the first place, those would be very good questions. Unfortunately that would take at least another interesting novel to describe, and it's beyond the scope covered here.

To get an idea of the magnitude of the US debt, I once saw a pictograph where *one trillion dollars was represented by a tall square column similar in size to the base and height of the Statue of Liberty.* Now imagine the Statue of Liberty standing tall in the middle, with 28 similar sized columns surrounding it each representing the 28 trillion dollars' worth of debt. By the way, *each of the 28 columns contained 1,000 pallets and each pallet held one billion dollars of crisp one-hundred-dollar bills.* The national debts of countries around the world are astounding to put it mildly.

With these mind-numbing debts in mind, accountability is certainly not a popular word when it comes to governments nor people in general. I certainly don't pretend to understand how exactly the national debts will ever be dealt with in the short term nor long term. However, looking at history, it's safe to assume that they will introduce some scheme to inform us average folks that the debt is not that big of a problem after all. We'll be told that we really don't have anything to worry about because they have it *all under control.* Nothing to see here, so let's just keep it moving without any commonsense questions. After all, they will need to borrow a bit more for a little while longer, trying to downplay it as much as possible. It just feels like smoke and mirrors.

It's clear that they just want to keep spending more money than the amount coming in. They will also introduce doubt regarding the debt not being a problem at all just in case someone questions it. They want to project the illusion of confidence, so they'll come up with anything, even if it sounds too good to be true. What is painfully obvious is that the value of each dollar in circulation is getting killed as time moves forward and the national debt continues to balloon out of control. We all know that everything costs more as each dollar continues its downward spiral in real purchasing power. That is the bottom line which cannot be denied.

On an individual level, what would happen if someone were to continue to accumulate more and more debt year after year?

What if you maxed out every single credit card you have? If you had no savings, would you continue to apply for more credit cards so you can keep buying stuff with money you don't have? How long would you be able attain credit so you can continue to spend more than you earn? Along the way, some credit companies might even try to introduce doubt into your mind that your debt accumulation wasn't that big a problem. I mean, let's just keep the debt coming because you're not buried up to your eyeballs in debt just yet.

Debt + Doubt = Death

If left unchecked, debt is a silent killer. It is a disease. If left untreated, debt is deadly both physically and spiritually. It will eat you up from the inside out. All debt will eventually be paid by someone. You may be able to work your way toward paying off your physical debt, or perhaps you may win the lottery, or you may get a big bonus from your work, or you may receive an inheritance, or someone you have a relationship with will be kind enough to pay your money debt. Bottom line is that all debt will be paid for in the end. There are no exceptions.

Sin is another form of debt, but it has much greater eternal negative consequences. If this form of sin debt is left untreated, it is guaranteed to result in eternal spiritual death. The bad news is that sin is the kind of debt you will never be able to pay off with any amount of money. You will also never be able to pay for your sin debt on your own merits, no matter how good you are, and no matter what you do.

Everyone including those who do not have any physical money-type debt suffers from and is responsible for sin-type debt. The good news is that the sin-type of debt has already been paid for by the only One who could ever accomplish this. Sin-type debt was already covered in full by Jesus, God's only Son. Those who trust in Jesus owe nothing as their sin debt was already paid in full.

Satan, doing what he does best, will continue to introduce doubt when it comes to both types of debt. He will continue to seduce you into thinking that both your money-type debt as well as your sin-type debt are not really that bad. He will try to convince you that the sin debt problem isn't even real. He will continue to want to keep you in moral and spiritual darkness by introducing all kinds of doubt. He wants to keep you blind to the truth of its deadly consequences.

Knowing you're in debt is not a good feeling on any level. Again, I'm referring to the dangers of unmanageable physical money-type debt, as well as the eternal negative consequences of sin-type debt. There are mortal permanent dangers in store if you allow yourself to be deceived by doubt, blinding you to not recognize that all debt will need to be reconciled. You must recognize that you will be completely dependent on God to have your sin-type debt paid on your behalf. Having doubt about the reality of debt is a sure way for the money-type debt to keep you in bondage here on earth, and for you to end up paying for your sin-type debt by spending eternity in the lake of fire.

It is simply against the laws of nature to not pay for your debt. All debt will be paid for one way or another. There is no doubt about it so be on guard and don't allow yourself to be deceived. You might think you would get away with not paying your physical money-type debt if you happen to die while in debt. You might think the government will just absorb it or it might just evaporate somehow. The truth is that ultimately taxes will go up or prices for goods and services will go up for those still alive. Somebody will always end up paying for all physical money-type debt. When it comes to your sin-type debt, it also must be reconciled to God. Either you will trust in Jesus who has already paid for it, or you will pay for it yourself in eternity hell. That's about as real as it gets.

Biblical Truth from Chapter #7

There is no doubt that all physical money debt and all sin debt must be accounted for.

What do you personally think because it matters? When it comes to physical debt, it's a given that you're responsible for that. When it comes to sin debt, where do you stand on this subject? Do you believe that your personal sin debt has been paid in full by Jesus Himself? Are you willing to write it down and put your name on it? Are you tempted to minimize or discount it altogether? Are you allowing doubt to disguise the truth?

Nobody is above God's law because He is perfectly just, and all debt must be reconciled. If you still have doubt, then commit to taking the steps needed to gain understanding while you can. There is nothing more comforting than having the assurance of being spared from the devastation of the future things to come.

CHAPTER 8

Left Behind

There were only 29 likes when I stumbled across it one day. After watching the YouTube video, I pressed the thumbs up button to make it #30. I had just watched the eulogy for the late professional golfer Payne Stewart delivered by his friend and fellow pro golfer Paul Azinger. As Paul approached the podium of a large, packed church auditorium, he proceeded by first tucking the bottom of his slacks in his fancy knee-high socks to resemble the socks and knickers that Payne was famous for wearing on the golf course. Then Paul put on the recognizable flat cap-type hat that Payne was also known for.

Even if you're not a golfer, I think you would thoroughly enjoy this exceptionally moving video if you were so inclined to look for it and have a look. There is no doubt in my mind that most people would want those kinds of things said of us at our eulogy. I really don't know how Paul held it together. It was obvious that they had become close friends over the years. Paul described the time when he had been diagnosed with cancer. He mentioned that his friend Payne was the one who immediately gravitated toward him to support and encourage him during that difficult time.

Among other endearing memories Paul shared with the audience, I took note of one where Paul mentioned a time when the two of them were having dinner together. They had engaged in a deep conversation because Payne's father had just passed away. Payne was sharing his grief, and now Paul was the one lending an ear to his friend. Paul went on to assure and comfort Payne by saying *"We're not in a land of the living going to a land of the dying. We're in a land of the dying going to a land of the living."* These words meant a lot to Payne at that time, and they should matter to all of us today.

Both Paul and Payne were believers in God. Paul was sad that he had lost a close friend, but he was happy because he knew that his friend was now in heaven. Earlier that year, Payne had just won the US Open Golf Championship on Father's Day in June 1999 in spectacular fashion. He made a 15-foot putt on the last hole to win the tournament. I recall that Sunday afternoon vividly. I was going in and out of the house during an outdoor family gathering, and I got to witness one of the most memorable, dramatic finishes in PGA history.

It's also worth mentioning that during the US Open trophy presentation, Payne's first remarks were *"I want to first of all give thanks to the Lord because if it wasn't for the faith I have in Him, I wouldn't have been able to have the faith in myself on the golf course today."* Payne was not ashamed to declare who was behind the golf talent. He publicly declared on TV's biggest platform in golf that God was guiding his life in everything he did. God had transformed Payne's heart and he possessed an inner peace that surpassed all understanding.

Tragically, later in October of the same year Payne died in an unfortunate plane crash. His sudden, unexpected death obviously affected Payne's family and friends as well as the entire golf community who were left behind. It made national news. This larger-than-life person, husband and dad was suddenly gone from our midst.

Any one of us who have lived long enough can likely relate to some degree when we lose a loved one or a close friend or perhaps someone who we looked up to in some way. I know the feeling all too well with the sudden passing of my little sister during a horrific car crash which I happen to have survived. She was only 18 years old at the time and I was 21. I was also comforted beyond words because my little sister was also a believer in God. I knew for sure that her soul ended up in heaven that fateful night. There was no doubt in anyone's mind who knew her that she was a Christian. For one reason or another, some people end up passing away even younger, while others leave us at a much older age. There is an understandable feeling of loss when someone in our immediate circle of influence dies, and we get left behind.

What if someone you knew was to suddenly disappear without a trace? I don't mean disappear as in going away or hiding somewhere, but instead as in literally disappearing off the face of the earth. Just imagine you were walking and talking with a friend and while in mid-sentence, your friend was no longer there next to you. Maybe you would think that it was a trick of some sort, so you end up going to your friend's house hoping to find him there. Once you arrive, you only find your friend's dad who now tells you the bizarre account of his wife also having just disappeared while they were talking. What would you possibly make of it? Your friend and his mom are both suddenly gone and you're looking for clues as to what may have happened.

You and your friend's dad are understandably worried trying to make sense of what you both experienced. To make matters worse, you notice the television running in the background making emergency announcements and breaking news alerts. You're also now being texted Amber alerts on your cell phone constantly for missing kids. Every single channel is reporting news of all kinds of chaos and confusion happening everywhere. Unexplained car crashes, trains, planes and bus accidents along with horrible industrial incidences are all over the news. The madness is all taking place across the globe because people have disappeared seemingly as a coordinated effort.

Whether previously playing sports, or driving, or boating, or working, or walking, or sleeping, people were being reported to have simply vanished without explanation. There was nothing but chaos, grief, confusion and panic everywhere. Government officials were desperately coming on the air trying to calm things down and establish some semblance of order but without success. The news was bleak, and the markets were tanking. The common theme being reported was that some people were simply gone in an instant, while the majority were left behind without any warning or explanation. What in the word could possibly be going on here?

In short, the scenario described above is a likely one and can certainly play out during *The Rapture*. This has obviously not taken place yet. The rapture is the biblical doctrine referring to a time when all true believers, both dead and living, will be snatched up off the face of the earth. It is the time when the Lord Jesus, God's son will gather those who believe to Himself in heaven where they will all receive their glorified bodies being united with their souls.

> *For the Lord Himself will descend from heaven with a shout, with the voice of an archangel, and with the trumpet of God. And the dead in Christ will rise first.* (1 Thessalonians 4:16)
>
> *Then we who are alive and remain shall be caught up together with them in the clouds to meet the Lord in the air. And thus we shall always be with the Lord.* (1 Thessalonians 4:17)
>
> *Therefore comfort one another with these words.* (1 Thessalonians 4:18)

The rapture is indeed an event of comfort for those who believe, but it is an event of terror for those left behind. Just as sure as supernatural creation of the universe took place at some point in the past, the rapture of believers will also take place according to God's sovereign timeline at some point in the future. God, The Father is the only one who knows when this will happen, and it will be during a time when folks will be least expected. Just prior to that pre-appointed time, things will appear to be completely *normal* to the average person so it will seem to have come out of nowhere.

The rapture will be quick and abrupt, and everyone all over the globe will know it because they will have been left behind. They will realize that they didn't make it. This single event will be the most dramatic and noteworthy in post-modern history. It will cause sheer panic across the world in unimaginable ways and will set into motion the next set of terrifying things to come during the following seven-year period. The rapture of believers along with the immediate events to follow will mark the end of this era and will usher in the next age to come.

So, given that we don't know the exact date, are we at least getting close to the time of the rapture? Do we have any clues? Every generation since the death and resurrection of Jesus has anticipated this event and rightfully so, but it has not happened yet. As a result, people have been increasingly complacent that things will continue just the way they have been. People have deliberately pushed God away at every turn and most even mock the idea of a rapture being imminent. The fact that people in general are discounting this future event to come is irrelevant but noteworthy, nonetheless.

We can all take note of the world events around us and we ought to be ready. Every world leader is appointed according to God's grand design, and none rise to their position by accident. Everything happens for a reason, so we need to pay attention. With the recent rise of the internet being placed in the palm of most everyone on the planet, it's reasonable to conclude that most have either already heard about the true God and His plan for redemption, or that they will very soon. Once that happens, we are one more step closer. And yes, there are plenty of additional clues that the end times of this era we live in are approaching faster than ever.

If we observed the buds appearing on trees, then we obviously don't need to research what comes next because we already know. We believe that spring and summer are just around the corner. In the same way, we are given cluses through God's word, the Holy Bible, of what comes next for all of humanity. Witnessing these astonishing signs to which we can pay attention and watch for, we can conclude that we're getting closer to the time of the rapture.

In the end times, the end of this era we're in now, Jesus compares that period with the days of Noah and Lot where people were doing eight specific activities just prior to the catastrophic events that took place. People were eating, drinking, marrying, giving in marriage, buying, selling, building, and planting. Nothing seemingly out of the ordinary was going on. These things took place up until the day Noah and his family entered the Ark. Then the flood came, and God destroyed everything, and everyone left behind outside the ark. This major event marked the end of that era where the atmosphere changed drastically. Nothing lived as long after the flood.

Similar kinds of activities were going on in the days of Lot. But on the day when Lot and his family left Sodom as he was instructed, fire and sulfur rained down from heaven, and God had destroyed everyone who was left behind in the city. Wow! Some might think that was quite extreme. With all the seemingly *normal* activities going on previously, what could have triggered such a reaction from God? There is a limit to His patience, but He is also just by His very nature.

Everyone except Noah and his family was wiped off the face of the earth during the flood. Everyone except Lot and his family were destroyed by fire in the city of Sodom. Why would Jesus give us this clue and compare the end times of this age with that of Noah and Lot? What was similar and what is He bringing to our attention for us to watch for and be aware of?

They didn't want to recognize the last days in which they were living. They ignored God's warnings. They were full of pride. They were mostly concerned about stuff known in our days as materialism. They grew increasingly distant to God Himself and had no regard for the spiritual and the eternal things. They pushed away God's laws and gave in to all kinds of fleshly desires and sins. They became increasingly wicked from the inside out. They became impatient with everything and flat out unruly even in their imagination and thoughts.

> *Then the Lord saw that the wickedness of man was great in the earth, and that every intent of the thoughts of his heart was only evil continually.* (Genesis 6:5)

What appeared to be going on as *normal* as far as the eight activities of eating, drinking, marrying, giving in marriage, buying, selling, building, and planting, there was a whole lot of evil and godlessness brewing beneath the surface of it all. People were becoming increasingly and universally corrupt and deceitful even in their thoughts. Everything had been poisoned by doubt.

They lacked respect, were shameless, did not value life, and they worshiped false gods and images. They introduced unfiltered practices that were contrary to God's natural design such as marriage, among others. They were full of themselves and full of pride. It's also worth mentioning they built the tower of Babel to reach heaven because they wanted to show off.

> *And they said, "Come, let us build ourselves a city, and a tower whose top is in the heavens; let us make a name for ourselves, lest we be scattered abroad over the face of the whole earth." (Genesis 11:4)*

Does this sound familiar at all? Does it resemble our modern culture which is proposing to build mile-high buildings and gargantuan structures to house populations of entire cities and countries in them? During the days prior to the ensuing destruction in the days of Noah and Lot, the earth was filled with all kinds of corruption. People continued to descend lower resorting to violence, rebellion, theft, deception, rudeness, selfishness, idolatry, lack of self-control, immorality, carnality, defiance, and pride. They ignored God's warnings then, and it sure looks like they're ignoring them now.

Noah and Lot both received supernatural revelation of what was about to happen on the earth and how they can prepare for it, face it and survive. In our current environment, we too are confronted with enormous dangers, natural disasters, false teachings, and similar circumstances the sum of which we cannot fully measure nor appreciate. What is safe to conclude is that there has been a gradual spiritual and moral decline as of late, and God is warning us of these end times through His Word.

> *However, when He, the Spirit of truth, has come, He will guide you into all truth; for He will not speak on His own authority, but whatever He hears He will speak; and He will tell you things to come.* (John 16:13)

We have all been shown what to look for and we all know what is needed to survive and fulfill God's purpose just as He has clearly indicated. We have been shown what is about to take place next, and the conditions seem to be lining up. The Holy Spirit has revealed this to us just as He had done with Noah. We are expected to stay alert, take note of what is happening around us, and not be deceived nor be afraid. We need to rest assured and heed God's warnings of what is to come next as we are clearly approaching the end of this age. Nobody knows the exact time, but the Rapture of believers is definitely the next event on God's sovereign timetable. We need to be prepared so that we do not get left behind. I recently heard a phrase from the pastor at our church and it's worth emphasizing.

No faith, know fear .... Know faith, NO fear.

Biblical Truth from Chapter #8

The Rapture of believers in Jesus Christ will happen soon, while non-believers will be left behind.

What do you personally think because it matters? When it comes to the Rapture of all believers from earth to heaven marking the beginning of the end of this era, where do you stand on this subject? Given all the current world events as well as all human pride on full display everywhere, are you tempted to just ignore the facts as well as Jesus' warnings? Do you personally believe the Rapture will happen? More importantly, do you believe you will be included, or will you be left behind? Are you willing to write it down and put your name on it?

If you're reading this but are still skeptical, there is still hope. Take the steps needed to gain understanding until you're sure. There is nothing more comforting than having the assurance of being spared from the devastation of the seven-year period following the Rapture as well as the subsequent things to come.

CHAPTER 9

SEVEN-YEAR TRIBULATION PERIOD

If you end up being one of those left behind after the rapture, it will feel like a movie and likely a nightmare. Unfortunately for you, it will be as real as it gets, and about to get more intense. Once the rapture of the believers takes place, you will look around and you will call people to get your bearings as to what just happened. It will be difficult at best for you to process the events you will witness. People you have known for years will be gone and you will not be able to reach them.

You will dig deep into your memory banks and recall that there was something different about those individuals who are no longer around. You will remember that they have tried to talk with you on occasion about God and creation and Jesus as being the only way to heaven. You might even recall conversations regarding the end times and how it would play out. You had ignored it all along, and you will realize that you were left behind. The rapture of believers had just taken place, and you will be faced with the grim reality that the beginning of the end of this era has just begun.

I'll be the first to admit that it's very difficult to describe anyone's specific reaction to the events following the rapture as it has not happened yet. The scenario unfolding in the beginning paragraphs of this chapter is what I suspect would be a reasonable one taking place. If you are still alive at that time and find yourself having missed the rapture, you will quickly be bombarded with instructions from government officials as well as practically everyone around you. They will be busy trying to restore order across the globe and will likely issue directives requiring total compliance.

No questions allowed, and certainly no mention of the reality of God, the evident rapture itself, or anything to do with Jesus. Don't believe anything you've just witnessed, just listen to what we're telling you because it's for your own good. This will come as no surprise because everyone left behind after the rapture will be non-believers. Some folks will realize their huge mistake and they will experience true regret, remorse, and even repentance. Most will become even more defiant, continuing to curse God at every opportunity, especially for leaving them behind.

The main message being discussed by the talking heads on TV during that time will likely have a spin revolving around *national security* and everyone just needs to fall in line. Just do as you're told. The powers that be will want to portray a sense that they've got it all together and it will be okay as long as everyone cooperates. Compliance will be mandatory. No more tolerance for individual suggestions such as *maybe we should turn to God and ask for His mercy.* One world order will likely be popular among the masses during that time.

The book of Revelation is the last book of the Bible, and it is perhaps the most misunderstood, most misinterpreted, and most neglected of all the others. It is in this last book where God reveals the next events that will take place in the end times. He wants us to know the things to come to fulfill His messianic timeline for all of humanity and no one will be able to claim ignorance.

> *Blessed is he who reads and those who hear the words of this prophecy and keeps those things which are written in it; for the time is near.* (Revelation 1:3)

> *Behold, I am coming quickly! Blessed is he who keeps the words of the prophecy of this book.* (Revelation 22:7)

The seven-year period following the rapture of the believers is known as the Tribulation Period or the Great Tribulation. Revelation chapters 6 through 19 describe the horrific events about to unfold on planet earth. During this time, God's judgment and His wrath will be poured out onto unbelieving and rebellious humanity in the fullest measure. This will be a period where most Jewish people as well as many from other nations will turn back to God, although they will endure many hardships and even death. It will be a period of retribution, redemption, and restoration. It will set the stage for the triumphant second coming of Jesus Himself to set up His millennial kingdom to follow.

This seven-year Tribulation period can be characterized as a time of great destruction, a time of reckoning, a time of elimination of idolatry, a time of inescapable judgment for unbelieving man, and a time for the remnant few, both Jews and Gentiles, to turn to God. This period is described in sequence as God's sovereignty, power, and justice comes into full view.

The scene begins in heaven where God handed a sealed scroll to His son, Jesus, who was the only one capable and worthy to open it. The rapture had just taken place and the believers were already with Him in heaven at this point. Jesus was about to take full control of the earth by unrolling the scroll as a title deed, opening the seals, one at a time. The scroll was sealed with seven seals each of which revealed something new and the total time it took for all of this to unfold was the seven years known as The Tribulation period as follows:

- ▷ The scroll was sealed with seven seals identifying *The Seven Seal Judgments.*
- ▷ The seventh seal revealed seven trumpets identifying *The Seven Trumpet Judgments.*
- ▷ The seventh trumpet revealed seven bowls to be poured out as *The Seven Bowl Judgments.*

Seal Judgment #1 – This represents a time of *False Peace*. Revealed is a *white horse* with a rider holding a bow but no arrows. This will be a conqueror who will conquer without the need for war. It has been suggested that this will be the Antichrist establishing himself because of his great influence in the world at the time. There will be peace on earth after the rapture, but it will be a false peace energized by the popular Antichrist. He will be a false Christ, and he will make a pact with the people to establish peace on earth which would not last long.

Seal Judgment #2 – This represents a time of *Conflict and War*. Revealed is a *red horse* with a dominating force for disruption. Wartime will be prevalent on the earth as peacetime will have been short lived.

Seal Judgment #3 – This represents a time of *Scarcity and Famine*. Revealed is a *black horse* with a rider who had a pair of balances or scales in his hand. During this time, everything will need to be measured precisely. Scarcity and extreme famine will be prevalent on the earth.

Seal Judgment #4 – This represents a time of *Widespread Death*. Revealed is a *pale horse* with a rider whose name was Death. It makes sense that after war and famine comes death. This will be the fourth and last of *The Four Horsemen of the Apocalypse*. Power will be given to this one to bring death to 25% of the remaining world population.

Seal Judgment #5 – This represents the *Cry of the Martyrs*. Revealed are the voices of the souls of those who had been slain crying out to God in heaven to avenge their blood. There will be war and carnage on the earth during this time, especially against those who will resist the Antichrist. This period will mark the half-way point of the seven-year Tribulation period.

Seal Judgment #6 – This represents a time of *Cosmic Disturbances*. A great earthquake will erupt, the sun will become black, the moon will become like blood, stars will fall from heaven on the earth, the sky will be shaken and rolled up while mountains and islands will be moved from their place. Indescribable fear and sheer terror will engulf anyone left on earth as God's wrath will be unleashed like never before.

Seal Judgment #7 – There is some overlap here as this last seal contains the *Prelude to the Seven Trumpet Judgments* – There will be more thundering, lightnings, an earthquake and also silence in heaven for about a half hour. Every soul in heaven will be in complete awe regarding the holocaust of divine fury taking place on the earth during this time.

By the middle of this seven-year Tribulation period, there will be 144,000 Jews who will be spared. God will literally elect 12,000 Jews from each of the 12 tribes of Israel. During the chaos, they will be saved, believing that Jesus Christ is their Savior and Lord. There will be a great revival during this period as people will realize they had missed the rapture and were now left behind. The Jewish people from the tribes of Israel will mourn as they will recognize that they were the ones who originally crucified Christ as stated in Zechariah 12:10-14.

Through God's protection and the ministry of these 144,000 redeemed Jews, there will be an innumerable amount of people saved, yet many will still be martyred. This last seal judgment will release the seven trumpet judgments to follow as each one will be sounded in sequence.

Trumpet Judgment #1 – *Vegetation will be struck.* Hail and fire mixed with blood will be cast on the earth. One third of the trees and grass will be all burned up.

Trumpet Judgment #2 – *Seas will be struck.* A great mountain burning with fire, possibly a huge burning meteor or asteroid, will be thrown into the sea. One third of the sea will become blood-like, one third of the living creatures in the sea will die, and one third of ships out at sea will be destroyed.

Trumpet Judgment #3 – *Fresh waters will be struck.* A celestial body will fall on one third of the rivers and springs like a burning torch. One third of the fresh water will become bitter and poisonous and many more will die.

Trumpet Judgment #4 – *The heavens will be struck.* One third of the sun, one third of the moon, and one third of the stars will be darkened. As a result, one third of the light from day and night will be lost.

Trumpet Judgment #5 – *Locusts from the bottomless pit will be released.* A star unlike the celestial bodies in the sky will fall from heaven onto the earth. This will be an angelic being, likely Satan, and he will be given the key to the bottomless pit where demons were kept locked up. Once opened, smoke and demons in the form of locusts with the power of scorpions will come out of the pit. They will be ordered not to destroy any tree nor grass, nor kill anyone. Instead, they will sting and torment for five months all those who did not have God's seal and protection. During that time of agony, men will desire to die but death itself will flee from them.

Trumpet Judgment #6 – *The Four Angels from the Euphrates* *will be released.* These demonic angels and their armies numbering two hundred million will have been bound and kept for this precise time. They will now be released, and they will have fire, smoke, and brimstone coming out of their mouths. One third of the remaining population will be killed. The rest who were not killed by these plagues continue to curse God. They would still not repent for their worship of demons, idols, gold, silver, brass, stone, or wood which could neither see nor hear nor walk.

Trumpet Judgment #7 – *The Kingdom will be proclaimed, and seven bowl judgments will be next* – By this time, the nations will be filled with total defiant rage.

Other events of significance during this time will be that more of Satan's angels will be cast down to earth. The Antichrist will have great influence as the world ruler along with his cohort, the False Prophet. They will continue to deceive people incorporating *the mark of the beast,* without which life will be even more difficult during this time.

This mark of the beast will identify allegiance to the Antichrist, but it should be avoided and resisted at all costs, even to death. They will continue to pursue the destruction of Israel, but God will continue to provide protection for Israel and all His elect Jews and Gentiles. The seven bowl judgments to follow will be poured out in rapid-fire succession towards the very end of this seven-year Tribulation period.

Bowl Judgment #1 – *Loathsome sores will appear on people* from the pouring out of the first bowl on the earth. There will be a foul and painful sore on all those who had the mark of the beast and those who worshiped his image.

Bowl Judgment #2 – *The sea will turn to blood* when the second bowl will be poured out on the sea. The sea will become like blood and every living creature remaining in the sea will die.

Bowl Judgment #3 – *The waters will turn to blood* when the third bowl will be poured out on the rivers. All freshwater rivers and springs will turn to blood.

Bowl Judgment #4 – *Men will be scorched* when the fourth bowl will be poured out on the sun. The sun will become so hot it will scorch men with great heat while they still would not repent. God had the power over all these plagues, yet men will only blaspheme Him even more.

Bowl Judgment #5 – *Darkness and pain* from the fifth bowl will be poured out on the Antichrist and his entire kingdom. These plagues will all be cumulative with unimaginable suffering and painful outcomes.

Bowl Judgment #6 – *The Euphrates River will be dried up* from the pouring out of the sixth bowl on it. God will supernaturally dry up this river in the last days before the battle of Armageddon.

By this point, nations and their armies will gather there to perhaps rebel against the Antichrist whose failure to alleviate the world's suffering will erode his popularity. Or, perhaps they will gather there as a final attempt to destroy Israel in retaliation for Israel's God having sent all these plagues on them.

The hostility will reach the point of a final and foolish attempt to fight against Christ. This will be an obvious doomed, futile effort that will mark the apex of human rebellion against God. Unclean spirits like demons will come out of the mouths of the unholy trinity, Satan, the Antichrist, and the False Prophet as they will approach their final act.

Bowl Judgment #7 – *The earth will be utterly shaken* as the seventh and final bowl will be poured out into the air. In the midst of it all, out of heaven will come Jesus Christ as King of kings and Lord of lords. This will be His second return to earth, but this time it will be in a triumphant fashion. There will be noises, and thunder, and lightning, and an earthquake greater than ever before in human history. Islands will flee away, and mountains will be no more. Great blocks of hail will fall from heaven weighing about a hundred pounds each, indicating unparalleled atmospheric convulsions.

It will finally all be over. The remaining rebels will be overcome by Lord Jesus. The Antichrist and the False Prophet who deceived many into receiving the mark of the beast and worshiping his image will be captured. They will both be cast alive into hell, the eternal lake of fire burning with brimstone. Satan will be bound and tossed into the bottomless pit. Carnage, destruction, and death will be everywhere. God's wrath will have been unleashed on all unbelieving, unfaithful, unrepentant, idolatrous, immoral, prideful sinners. The end of this seven-year Tribulation period will mark the end of this era we are currently living in. The dawn of a new era will soon follow.

Biblical Truth from Chapter #9

The Seven-Year Tribulation Period will display God's wrath, and Jesus Christ will return to earth marking the end of this era.

What do you personally think because it matters? When it comes to the Seven-Year Tribulation period as described in the book of Revelation, where do you stand on this subject? Do you personally believe the end of our current era will end this way? Are you willing to write it down and put your name on it?

If you are skeptical now but find yourself having been left behind when the rapture occurs, you will still have hope. You will need to refuse the mark of the beast at all costs during this seven-year period. Better yet, you ought to investigate anything that is not yet clear while you have the opportunity in order to avoid God's wrath altogether. There is nothing more comforting than having the assurance of being spared from the devastation of the Seven-Year Tribulation period that is sure to take place after the rapture.

CHAPTER 10

1,000 Years + Eternal State = Forever End Game

Planet earth as we know it today will not be gone after the devastation it endures during the seven-year Tribulation period. Following that time of judgment, a new era lasting an additional one thousand years will have just begun. To say that this new era will be different than the one before would be a huge understatement. King Jesus will be in complete charge during this time, and He will reign supreme from Jerusalem. This is known as *The Millennial Period* or *The Millennial Kingdom of Jesus*.

Just as the atmospheric conditions were much different after the disturbance of the earth due to the great flood from Noah's time, so will conditions be much different after the disturbance of the earth due to the massive events that will take place during the Tribulation period. It will be a new era and everyone on the planet during this time will know that the rightful King Jesus reigns. There will be no misunderstanding about who is in charge during the millennial period. All people and creatures no longer lived as long after the devastation of the flood during Noah's time. Likewise, all life and creature behaviors will also be different after the devastation of the Tribulation period.

I will say up front that there have been countless books and commentaries related to the end times written by theologians and students of history and the Bible. I would strongly encourage you to continue your path to learning as much as you can until you're sure that this period of time is in fact coming our way. I will in no way claim that what I summarize in the next few paragraphs is complete in any way, shape or form. I will however assert that the Holy Bible, God's Word, is the only true source for what has been revealed on the subject.

We have all learned the Lord's prayer or at least we have heard about it. It's how the Lord Jesus taught us to pray to God the Father with the words *thy kingdom come, thy will be done on earth as it is in heaven*. It is this Millennial Kingdom on earth that we're asking God to bring to us where His will is to be done right here on earth as it is being done in heaven. Our prayers will be answered because God is faithful and true to His word. The Lord's prayer will come true. It will be this, the Lord's Millennial Kingdom right here on earth that will become reality for all to see. It's what all believers are asking for whenever we pray what Jesus Himself has taught us.

As a quick review, the *End Times* consist of the *Rapture*, the *Seven-Year Tribulation Period* and the *One-Thousand-Year Millennial Kingdom*. What follows after all that will be the *Eternal State* which is the *Forever* part. For now, we will just continue where we left off in the previous chapter.

The rapture of all believers to heaven will have taken place. As the Tribulation period got started, Lord Jesus, being the only one willing, able and worthy, had begun to open the scroll which God the Father in heaven had given to Him. The scroll was the title deed to the entire universe and Jesus was about to take it back as the rightful heir. God's wrath was unleashed on the celestial bodies, on the land and waters of the earth itself, and on the creatures as well as all rebellious mankind remaining on the earth at the time. This unimaginable punishment came by way of seven seal judgments, seven trumpet judgments, and seven bowl judgments.

At the end of this devastating seven-year Tribulation period, King Jesus will return from heaven to earth, only this time, triumphantly. The Antichrist and False Prophet will be defeated and cast alive into the eternal lake of fire burning with brimstone. As of that point, they will be in hell for all eternity. Satan will also be bound and thrown in the bottomless pit but only for the duration of the thousand-year millennial period.

The Millennial Kingdom and the new era will be inaugurated with this, Jesus's second coming to earth at the end of the seven-year Tribulation period. The others arriving with Jesus will be His angels as well as all the saints from all times. The saints will be in their resurrected glorified bodies. They will all descend from heaven following triumphant Jesus to earth.

Also, dwelling on the earth at the time will be the remaining human beings who will have survived. These will be the multitude of Jews and Gentiles who repented, were saved, were protected by God, and were still alive after all the Tribulation judgments had passed. Miraculously, a lot of people will have survived. Jesus Christ will rule over the whole earth for a one-thousand-year period as the promised Messiah.

The following are summary points and characteristics of the one-thousand-year Millennial Kingdom. It's worth noting who will be there during that time and in what form as the new era begins.

- ▷ Jesus Christ will reign on earth with complete authority over all nations from Jerusalem for one thousand years. In the millennium, the nation Israel will experience the blessing which God had promised to Abraham and David pertaining to Israel's land, nationality, and throne.
- ▷ Jesus' reign will be worldwide, and He will be recognized as King of kings and Lord of lords. Jesus will be the only One to bring peace to the Middle East, unlike anyone else throughout history.
- ▷ Satan will remain bound and chained up in the abys, the bottomless pit. His activity on earth will come to an abrupt halt and he will be completely powerless for this entire one-thousand-year period. Only after the millennium's completion will he be released, but only for a short period.

- Angelic beings from heaven will dwell on earth during the millennium. They will have descended to earth following Jesus at His triumphant second coming.
- All saints of all ages will reign with Jesus on earth during this one-thousand-year period. These are the believers of all time who had died prior to the Rapture. They will have been resurrected from the dead in glorified bodies and joined with their souls in heaven at the Rapture. This is known as the first resurrection. These saints in glorified bodies will have descended to earth with Jesus at His second coming.
- All the believers who were alive and were caught up at the Rapture and received glorified bodies will also reign on earth during the millennium. These saints will also return to earth with Jesus at His second coming.
- All the martyrs who were converted to believe but were killed during the devastating seven-year Tribulation period. These saints in glorified bodies will also return to earth with Jesus at His second coming to reign for the millennium period.
- All the remaining human beings still alive, the Jews and Gentiles who did not take the mark of the beast, will remain on earth and simply transition directly into the millennial kingdom. They will have survived the seven-year Tribulation period and will remain as human beings on earth to begin the new era. It's worth noting that these human beings will *not* have glorified bodies when entering the millennium period. They will still be human beings who had just witnessed all the

power and wrath of holy God on sinful mankind, and yet survived. They will have witnessed the triumphant return of Jesus to earth coming from the clouds along with His angels and saints following Him.

- Being on earth during Jesus' millennial reign will be a great blessing to all inhabitants. It will be a time of unparalleled justice. This period will be described as peaceful, joyful, ethical, spiritual, moral, righteous, prosperous, socially beneficial, and religiously pure where everyone will worship King Jesus. It will mark a time of physical health and wellbeing leading to long life for all remaining human beings. Death will also be limited due to atmospheric conditions having been altered considerably from those of today.
- Animal behaviors and social conditions will also be transformed during the one-thousand-year reign of the Prince of Peace, Jesus Himself. Conditions of peace will prevail unlike ever before.
- *The wolf also shall lie down with the young goat, the calf and the young lion and the fatling together; And a little child shall lead them. The cow and the bear shall graze; Their young ones shall lie down together; And the lion shall eat straw like the ox. The nursing child shall play by the cobra's hole, and the weaned child shall put his hand in the viper's den.* (Isaiah 11:6-9)

I totally get it. Given our current state as mere mortal human beings, we have limited understanding of many things. It's hard to imagine seeing a You Tube channel showing a child playing with a cobra, or a wolf sleeping next to a goat without any harm done, or a lion eating straw. It's not a normal part of this era we're in at the moment so we can't really relate to the next one to come. It's worth noting that the previous era, the one before Noah's flood, was such that people lived to be 900 years old and animals grew to be gigantic dinosaurs. Likewise, we also don't really understand with any totality what it was like during that era, the one before the flood.

So, it's safe to say that we do not fully understand the future eras to come because we're not used to seeing or observing those sorts of things. Granted, we also have to admit that we don't understand what makes the sun continue to burn while maintaining its perfect distance from us in this day and age. It's a given, however, that we are convinced and are glad of the presence of these invisible forces needed for our existence, nonetheless.

All conditions of the next era on this earth, the Millennial period following the seven-year Tribulation period, will be vastly different than those we experience today. Long life for human beings will prevail during that time. Death will still happen, but not nearly as early in age as we currently experience. All saints in their glorified bodies as well as all angels will remain on earth during the millennium interacting with the human beings. The atmosphere as well as the relationships between the inhabitants of the earth and animals will be extremely different during the new era. We certainly don't know all of the intricate details, but we know enough through what has been revealed to us by God Himself. We have been given a glimpse into His plan for all of humanity moving forward.

At the end of the millennium, there will be one more final battle between good and evil, as an exclamation point to this one-thousand-year period. To demonstrate that even in a near perfect environment with no interference or temptation from Satan for one thousand years, man in human form will still be capable of rebellion against God. As remarkable as this may sound, this is what is revealed and can be expected to take place at the end of this millennial period.

At the beginning of the millennium, we reviewed that there will be two types of persons on the earth. There will be the believers with glorified bodies who were resurrected from the dead, as well as the believers with non-glorified bodies as human beings who survived the Tribulation period. These believers in human form can and will have children. Although they will have longer lives, these human beings and their descendants, like all persons, will have the opportunity to say yes or no to Jesus. Out in the open, it will appear that they will say yes. However, over time in their hearts, sadly many will say no and reject Jesus' authority.

Over time, these human beings may even begin to question and introduce doubt about the reality of the devastating previous Tribulation period. That would not be surprising as there are people today who also question the great flood that happened during Noah's time. They will have a false and useless confession of faith just as many do today. They will not hesitate to take any opportunity and rebel against the most amazing leader the world will have ever known. Their doom will be sealed even before the rebellion begins. Nothing will ever escape God's notice; not even what man thinks he is hiding in his heart. The curse on man will be *reversed* in the Millennium, but *it will not be removed completely* until the eternal state.

At the end of the one-thousand-year period, Satan will be released from the bottomless pit for one last time. He will bring leadership to the rebel human descendants born to the believers who first entered the millennium kingdom in human form. These rebels would be the children and future offspring of the ones who were converted to believe and survived the Tribulation period, then entered this new era with non-glorified human bodies. Satan will be let loose to reveal the true character of all Christ-rejecting human sinners who will be brought into judgment for the last time ever.

Satan will continue to do what he has always done; that is to lie and deceive. He is consumed now, and he will always be consumed with evil intentions. This has always been Satan's nature. He will deceive and gather the innumerable human rebels to do battle against King Jesus and to dethrone Him. They will also gather to destroy the other believers from Jerusalem and from all the surrounding area. Sinful humanity will demonstrate utter foolishness once more.

This time, the battle will be swift and final. At the end of this millennia era, fire will come down from God out of heaven and all the rebellious human unbelievers will be consumed instantly. Satan will be cast into the lake of fire and brimstone where the Antichrist and False Prophet had been for the past thousand years. It's the place where the unholy trinity will be tormented forever and ever.

It is at the end of this Millennial period, when all the unbelievers of all ages will be brought to experience a second death.

This will be a resurrection of condemnation for unbelievers. All deceased unbelievers from all ages will be resurrected at this point to be joined with their souls which had been in a state of pain all along. They will be required to stand at the Great White Throne of Judgment where they will be found unequivocally guilty by God in the person of Jesus Himself. No more chances. They will all be transformed with the type of eternal bodies to experience a second death by being cast into hell, the lake of fire, forever. Their torment will be literal, mental, physical and eternal with no reprieve, nor relief.

The Great White Throne of Judgment will only be experienced by unrepentant non-believers. This final judgment will happen during a short period between the end of the Millennial Kingdom and the Eternal State which is about to begin. At this point all the unbelieving sinners of all the ages, both demons and men, including Satan, the Antichrist, and the False Prophet will be in hell, the eternal lake of fire forever.

> *For the wrath of God is revealed from Heaven against all ungodliness and unrighteousness of men, who suppress the truth in unrighteousness.* (Romans 1:18)

At the end of the millennial period, after the final battle with Satan and the unbelievers, the entire universe as we know it today will be destroyed by God Himself. He will then create a new universe to be the eternal dwelling place of all the redeemed from all ages. God will create a *New Heaven* and a *New Earth* and a *New Jerusalem* that will last forever. It's worth noting that this existing universe we are currently a part of which God had created in the beginning is a temporary one. This current universe will have survived the era from Adam and Eve to Noah's flood, the current era we're in now since after the flood, and also the future millennial era. God has revealed to us that His future new creation will be a permanent one.

This new creation of a *New Heaven and New Earth* will be the *Eternal State* and it will continue this way forever. This will be the time when the *curse on man will have been removed for good*. The *New Environment* of the New Heaven and New Earth will have a completely different climate yet again. It will not be water based as we're told that there will be no more sea. All the believer saints from previous times, those from the time of the Tribulation, and those converted during the Millennial Kingdom make up the ultimate redeemed *Bride of Christ*. They will all dwell in the new creation, the New Jerusalem forever. There will be no more tears and God will be among them.

It has always been about God's plan and His elect people from Abraham, Isaac, Jacob, all the way to Jesus and the elect Gentiles of all nations. It's the reason why there has been conflict in the Middle East for as long as anyone can remember. During the millennial period, Israel will finally experience peace, and Jerusalem will be the place where Jesus Himself will rule over all nations of the earth during that era. Jerusalem, right here on earth, will be a lighthouse to the whole world for one thousand years with Jesus as King. However, the New Jerusalem will be the capital of the new creation in the future Eternal State where all the redeemed will be able to walk on streets of gold for all eternity thereafter.

Biblical Truth from Chapter #10

The 1000-year Millennial Kingdom of Jesus on this earth, followed by the Eternal State of heaven and hell define the END GAME. It is as final and AS REAL AS IT GETS.

What do you personally think because it matters? When it comes to the one-thousand-year Millennial Kingdom period as described in the book of Revelation, where do you stand on this subject? Do you believe this will be the next era where Jesus will reign as King over all nations? What about the Eternal State to follow and the ultimate destinations of believers, non-believers, and Satan? Do you personally believe this is how all of humanity will end? Are you willing to write it down and put your name on it?

If you want to learn something that is deep, then you must be willing to dig deep until you find it. If you are still skeptical while reading these words, your only hope is to humble yourself and ask God to open your eyes and soften your heart. There is nothing more comforting than having the assurance of spending eternity in heaven after you die.

_____

_____

_____

_____

CHAPTER 11

RECOGNITION + REMORSE + REPENTANCE = REDEMPTION

From a personal point of view, the writing of this third and final book has been more difficult than the first two. This may come across as a sort of complaint, but nothing could be further from the truth. As I'm now in the final chapter, I can definitely say that it's been a rewarding experience, and I have been blessed by it for sure. My heart is overflowing with gratitude and I'm thankful for every breath I take. I simply wanted to express that it was like an emotional rollercoaster, but one that I also feel extremely fortunate to have willingly taken.

Thinking, praying, researching, and writing about the end times brought me to a point of greater appreciation for where we are as a society currently, how quickly we seem to be approaching the last innings of this era, as well as the hope we all still have. I'm glad I got to experience all the twists and turns along the way, and I'm hopeful that you will be blessed and rewarded for having come along for the ride.

The most selfish thing you can do in this life is to help someone else. It's a gift you give yourself. I believe you know what I mean because that's where the joy is. That's where success and rewards crisscross. I've heard it being said that *people don't really care how much you know, until they really know how much you care.* I agree. From the very beginning, my intention in writing was for the Holy Spirit to touch the reader's heart in a way that causes them to end up in heaven for all eternity.

God is holy and He is certainly patient, but sin is serious, and He will not tolerate sin and evil forever. The total depravity of mankind runs deeper than any of us can imagine. Even after the one thousand years under the reign of the gracious King Jesus in a peaceful environment, God demonstrates that sinful man will still follow the deceptions of Satan and rebel against God. Without humility, recognition of man's sinful nature, and faith in God's son Jesus having paid the price in full, sinful man will have zero chance of ending up in heaven. That's just the way it was designed from the very beginning.

> *I am the way, the truth, and the life. No one comes to the Father except through Me.* (John 14:6).

Those were the words of God's son, Jesus. Regardless of anything anyone has ever written, regardless of anyone's heritage, background, or color of their skin, regardless of anyone's beliefs about eternity, we all must agree that Jesus certainly left His mark in the world. I mean the calendar that is being used across the globe was set up a long time ago to remind us of Him every single day, unlike anyone else, ever.

All historical references with respect to time, as in BC / AD, are used to indicate what happened before and after Jesus Himself. To further prove the point that sinful man continues to try and move away from Jesus, the latest politically correct version for reference is BCE / CE as in *Before the Common Era / Common Era,* in an effort to move away from Christianity. You just can't make this stuff up. Rebellion against God was embedded in the human sinful nature since the fall of man in the Garden of Eden.

Just try and allow that to sink in for a minute. This was meant to be this way, and yet most people do not give it the consideration it deserves. This fact alone should speak volumes and all of mankind should take note. The BC / AD time reference was and still is a big deal. There is something significantly different and obviously unique about Jesus and Christianity. The entire globe celebrates His birth at Christmas as well as His death and resurrection from the dead at Easter.

Most religions in the modern world say we can fix ourselves. What Jesus says which is unique is, the only way to be fixed is to let God fix you and to also let God do it the way He designed it to be done. It requires the recognition that you need something that you do not possess, you cannot attain on your own nor give to yourself. You need to ask God for something which only He can give you. And, you need to have the humility to be able to do that.

A person who responds to Jesus comes to a sense of appreciation that what God offers as a gift is something that they cannot generate for themselves no matter what they do or how hard they try. They come to a place of understanding that Jesus is the only one who could do the things that a human being, or any false god simply cannot do. They come to trust by faith in Jesus alone as He is the only way into heaven.

I've heard it being said that *if you live your life against the grain of creation, you're bound to get a few splinters* along the way. Jesus had the greatest impact on the world by far. Throughout the centuries, we've had plenty of sages telling us how to live and what we need to do. We also had, and still have, *holy* men giving us more rules, more prescriptions, more rituals, more demands on us so we can supposedly live the good life and work our way into heaven. It needs to be said that no man should ever be referred to as holy, nor should any man allow himself to be called holy by any other man. Most televangelists continue to pump up this *feel good, prosperity gospel notion* to this very day. It's big business and we all need to be aware of false teachers and unsound doctrines.

The reporting and documentation of Jesus' life and resurrection did in fact change the world. The Roman Empire abandoned the worship of its many gods. During that time, many claimed Jesus as the only son of God based on what they witnessed. The calendar changed from BC to AD, marking a new age *Anno Domini* as in *Year of the Lord*, where Jesus' promise of life gave hope for peace during that time, now, and forever.

So, why did Jesus have such a lasting impact? I mean, we all know what we need to do to be good. If Jesus had been just another person piling on another set of demands, requirements, and moral rules on top of us, He would never have had the impact He had. The reason Jesus had the impact He had is because He said that *maintaining moral rules was NOT the way to get saved.*

Moral rules are not the solution to our main sin problem. The solution is that Jesus, as God Himself came down to us, became a human being and suffered the punishment that was due to us because we constantly break these moral rules all the time. In other words, Jesus was saying *I'm the One who has done something to reconcile you to a holy God.* He was also saying that anything you might try and do on your own to get access to God and heaven will be a waste of time so don't fool yourself, nor allow others to fool you.

> For God so loved the world that He gave His only begotten Son, that whoever believes in Him should not perish but have everlasting life. (John 3:16)

God is the one who reached out and gave His only Son, if you can try and wrap your mind around that. Only in Christianity does God come down and reaches to man. Everywhere else, man is trying to reach up somewhere which goes back to man trying desperately to seek and think that he can do it himself. Perhaps other false gods expect that of man. For some reason people want to try to do it themselves, or at least they think they can, no doubt due to prideful influence. Only in Christianity does God reach down for us and that is an enormous difference. God didn't only reach down, but He left heaven and came down to earth in human form as the Lord Jesus Christ, in order to prepare the only way for sinful man to be reconciled to God.

Every other religion basically says that there is something wrong. There is some kind of a problem we each face. The problem is that there is a gap between us and the divine and we need to be enlightened in some way. These other religions then give you a set of rules on how to fix it. You will need to do this kind of meditation, or you will need to have this particular special diet, or you will need to follow these rules, or you will need to perform these rituals, or you will need to think, say, and do this and that. They're all telling you what YOU need to do. They're all piling on more responsibilities and tasks on top of you.

Christianity is the only religion which tells you what God has already done to cross the gap and fix the God-man relationship. Christianity tells you how God has already fixed the sin problem which no man, nor any false god, could have possibly done. It's the only religion where God took on the task Himself by coming and fixing it for us so that we didn't have to do it. He already knew we couldn't do it no matter how hard we tried. It never was, nor could it have been up to us. It's what God has already done for us.

That's what is unique about Christianity, and that's what is unique about Jesus. If He were just another sage that walked the face of this earth giving you more rules, then why believe? How would you differentiate between the others, so why pay any attention to His words? We all know the golden rule and we also know that we do not keep it. We all know that we have our sense of inadequacy, inferiority, failure, guilt and so on.

We already know that we do not do what we should do and there are plenty of people reminding us of that. We do not need any more reminders of how good we need to be. What is unique about Christianity is that it is not one more set of rules. Instead, it is the solution to our God-man separation. It is not up to what you do. It is about you accepting and believing what God has already done for you.

What may be surprising is that when looking at Jesus' life and His mission on earth, there was only a modest emphasis on the poor and even on loving one another. These points were made, and they matter but they were not the most important feature of His main purpose. Jesus didn't say *I came to help the poor*. He said, *I came to seek and to save those who are lost, to give My life a ransom for many, to call sinners to repentance.* Now, when sinners properly repent, they do care for the poor and others as well. That's part of the Christian reaction, but it's not the main reason why Jesus came.

Jesus also promised to send the Holy Spirit to make possible the kind of life that He was offering.

> *The Helper, the Holy Spirit whom the Father will send in My name, He will teach you all things, and bring to your remembrance all things that I said to you.* (John 14:26)

> *Peace I leave with you, My peace I give to you; not as the world gives do I give to you. Let not your heart be troubled, neither let it be afraid.* (John 14:27)

The Holy Spirit is a gift. It is a sort of enablement that God gives us. It comes from God, and it enables the creature to connect to the Creator. Through the Holy Spirit, we are empowered and thus it enables the possibility of this God-man relationship to take place. This comes on top of what most people associate Jesus with, which is His sacrifice in death for sinful man. Jesus essentially said that His purpose was to give life in all its fullness as well as the gift of eternal life.

Is it too good to be true? Some will always find a reason to doubt while other say it's a reason to trust Him completely. Yes, it's a matter of faith and everyone should give careful consideration to the promises that Jesus made. So, if life matters, and if what Jesus said about life is true, then it all boils down to whether we accept or reject a life that is real and good as it was designed; A life that can make a difference for us now, right here on earth, and forever after. It's not a question of the magnitude of what God has already done because we know that too. It's a question of whether you recognize your sin problem, feel true remorse, and are humble enough to genuinely repent. As one of the pastors at our church stated it, *the heart of the matter is a matter of the heart.* I agree.

We all need to pay to have insurance for our health, property, and for driving our car. The liability is simply too great without it. We will need to have proof of this earthly insurance *before the incident* otherwise we will not be covered and life on earth can certainly take a turn for the worse. In a similar way, only with a gargantuan difference, Jesus has already paid for your eternal life insurance.

Recognizing you need this insurance plus having a humble heart full of remorse and repentance, all combine to produce true redemption and forgiveness from your sin. This forgiveness is the sort of spiritual insurance which is only available from Jesus Himself. It goes without saying that for those of us who want to end up in heaven, we will need this eternity-type spiritual insurance *before life on earth ends*. That's just the way it is.

Straight up, people do not like to be reminded that sin is something all human beings suffer from. Regardless of the type of sin, it is all sin in any minute quantity that separates us from God. Many will try and sugarcoat sin's ugly reality because after all, it may offend them. It's as if they don't really want to hear the truth. It's as if someone had advanced terminal cancer with only days to live, but they would rather hear that *it's not that bad*. Sin is very misunderstood and we as a society just don't get it. People look at the news where someone just shot a bunch of innocent folks for no apparent reason, and they think, *that's a sinner but not me*.

People are told too many times that they don't really sin. Instead, they're told that they just *make bad choices, or they have bad habits, or they suffer from sexual addictions, but they're not really sinners*. They claim they don't really want to pursue their own fleshly desires but somehow, *it's out of their control*. They claim they're not sinners under the influence of this world, but the fact is that *this world is giving them exactly what they want, which is not God.*

People have normalized sinful behavior. They claim they're not sinners nor influenced by the powers of the prince of the air, but the fact is *they love the power of the prince of the air.* After all, they *sometimes make mistakes just like everyone else.* The bible says that they're children of wrath. Satan has deceived them all, and the fact is that they're lost and living in darkness. The fact is that the light of truth is the only thing that can overcome the darkness.

> *Do you not know that the unrighteous will not inherit the kingdom of God? Do not be deceived. Neither fornicators, nor idolaters, nor adulterers, nor homosexuals, nor sodomites, nor thieves, nor covetous, nor drunkards, nor revilers, nor extortioners will inherit the kingdom of God. And such were some of you. But you were washed, but you were sanctified, but you were justified in the name of the Lord Jesus by the Spirit of our God.*
> (1 Corinthians 6:9-11)

The bad news is that we're all sinners. The amazing news is that no matter the kind of sin you happen to be suffering from, God alone is the answer for you. Note the part, *and such were some of you*, from the quote above. There is no greater news for anyone who wants to hear the truth, recognize they need help, express remorse, genuinely repents and asks Jesus for help and forgiveness. It's your only hope to reach heaven one day. This was applicable to those during biblical times, and it's applicable to us today.

Sharing with the people you care about God's exact words without sugarcoating them is showing them that you care. You want them to go to heaven. It is only God's Word which has the power to bring any sinner to the realization that God alone can help them overcome any sinful situation at all. God's Word may not be something that they want to hear, but it's something that they absolutely need to hear. The spirit of love and truth will always overcome the spirit of error.

Heaven is full of people who were all sinners, but they genuinely repented and are now in God's presence. There is nobody in heaven who wanted nothing to do with Him while here on earth. Without a relationship with God here on earth, they will simply not end up in heaven. There is a lack of desire to get to know the one and only true God, Creator of this universe. Just think of all the funerals you attended, and everyone lines up to say and hear nice things about the deceased who never wanted to be known as one of God's own. Suddenly, people are told that the deceased *is in a better place* spending eternity with the One they didn't even acknowledge while alive.

Sadly, most people really don't get this. We want to tailor and distort God's Word to fit our preference and situation, so we feel better. We rarely want to hear the way it was designed by God Himself. We don't really understand it, and as a result we don't appreciate how desperate we are for radical redemption from sin.

For the most part, we don't realize we need to be helped, and we certainly don't believe we need to be saved from eternal damnation. We think we just need some good advice about how to live a great life as a good person. If only we were to follow these ten steps, we would reduce our stress and have a happy life *because that's our problem*. If enough of us were to chant the same ten-step improvement tune, then it must be true.

If the unrepentant deceased sinner at his own funeral would be able to talk to those who came to mourn, what do you honestly think he or she would say about the place they ended up in? Do you think the deceased unrepentant sinner is looking down from up above, or up from down below? What advice do you think the deceased would have for everyone at the funeral? Controversial topics are difficult because we don't want to offend anyone. I get it. However, compromising the truth of the sin-problem message is just dangerous.

As an example, I've heard it being said that *the problem with racism is sin, not skin*. When was the last time you heard any of the media talking heads call racism sin? That statement is as true as calling out all kinds of other sin for what it is as well. It can and should be done honestly, but always in love.

> *Truly, these times of ignorance God overlooked, but now commands all men everywhere to repent, because He has appointed a day on which He will judge the world in righteousness by the Man whom He has ordained. He has given assurance of this to all by raising Him from the dead.* (Acts 17:30-31)

We all need to be right with God if our end goal is to be in heaven. We need to be aware of false teachers who have come along throughout the ages preying on anyone who has virtually lost all interest in the Rapture, the return of Christ, and the end times. The mockers will be preying on the impatience of believers by sheer ridicule saying that things will just continue in the same way as always. The truth is that evolution is only an excuse, atheism is only an excuse, agnosticism and the pretense of ignorance are all excuses to free up the sinner to continue indulging in his sinful ways.

The truth is that there are repentant saved sinners, and there are unrepentant unsaved sinners. Turning from sin toward Jesus is our only hope to experience the fullness of life here on earth. He is also the only way into heaven for us to be in God's presence after we die. The heart and soul of the good news gospel starts with one's understanding, recognition, and acceptance of their own personal guilt due to sin, then asking Jesus for forgiveness, and finally accepting His gift of salvation to eternal life. The following is an example of what a sinner's genuine prayer might sound like:

> *Dear Lord Jesus, I recognize that I am a sinner, and I believe that you are God's only Son who suffered and died in my place. I ask that You forgive me, come into my heart, and help me follow Your ways. I promise and commit to making you my Lord and Savior.*

With a humble heart and the recognition and acknowledgment of our sinful nature, true remorse, confession to Him, genuine repentance for sin, and faith in Jesus alone as personal savior, God is faithful to forgive, no matter what you've done. There will be no question about whose you are because God's fingerprints will be all over your life, and everyone will know it. You will also know it in your heart because you will no longer pursue those things that will tend to distance you from your savior, even though you will still be tempted.

> *That if you confess with your mouth the Lord Jesus and believe in your heart that God has raised Him from the dead, you will be saved.* (Romans 10:9)

> *For with the heart one believes unto righteousness, and with the mouth confession is made unto salvation.* (Romans 10:10)

Recognition + Remorse + Genuine Repentance = True Redemption

You will continue to grow in your understanding of the grandeur of who God is and you will gladly gravitate toward Him, and He will draw you in His direction. You will remember to be faithful and help others you care about, by being honest and by pointing them toward God Himself who had mercy on you as well. You will experience peace and joy and gladness in your heart like never before. You will look for opportunities to give God praise saying, *help me to be worthy to be called a Christian,* and gratitude will overflow from your inner being.

Thank You, Lord Jesus,

- For another day of grace.
- For being in our lives, whether we realize it or not, whether we admit it or not.
- For health, for every breath I take, and for family.
- For daily strength, courage, and assurance.
- For wisdom and understanding.
- For love and compassion in my heart for others.
- For patience when warranted and for Your daily guidance.
- For Truth by revelation through Your Word, the Holy Bible.
- For the power of prayer and Your gift of faith.
- For helping me to move forward no matter what, knowing You are in control of all situations.
- For helping me to trust and believe in You by not being afraid nor anxious for anything.
- For providing me the courage, opportunity, and guidance to point others toward You.
- For helping me humble myself before You, always and continuously.
- For remembering that we are but dust yet precious in Your sight.
- For Your immeasurable love and mercy to have saved me to everlasting life.
- For the precious relationship with You, the one and only True and Holy God.
- For the Holy Spirit who dwells in my heart.
- For the precious gift of salvation through Jesus Christ, providing me access to heaven.

Last words should be lasting words. As I close out this final chapter, I wanted to point out the way Paul Azinger ended the eulogy of his friend Payne Stewart during the funeral, as I also found his comments to be true and appropriate.

> **Whoever you are, wherever you are, whatever you have done, if you feel the tug of God's Spirit on your heart, do not turn away.**

> *The Lord bless you and keep you;* (Numbers 6:24)

> *The Lord make His face shine upon you, and be gracious to you;* (Numbers 6:25)

> *The Lord lift up His countenance upon you, and give you peace.* (Numbers 6:26)

> **May God, Creator of all that exists, draw you near to Him, and into His eternal heaven.**
> **It is the END GAME and it is AS REAL AS IT GETS.**

Biblical Truth from Chapter #11

The forever after in eternity heaven is reserved for the genuine repentant sinners for whom Jesus died.

What do you personally think because it matters? When it comes to access to heaven and God through faith in Jesus alone, where do you stand on this subject? Do you believe? Have you prayed the sinner's prayer? Do you have a genuine personal relationship with God Himself? Are you willing to write it down and put your name on it?

If you want to know and really feel the happiness, freedom, and peace that only Jesus Christ can provide, then you are invited to look inside you heart, confess your sin, ask for forgiveness and receive Him as your Lord and Savior. Regardless of where you are or how you got there, know beyond the shadow of a doubt that His love for you is more than you can possibly imagine. Jesus' sacrifice satisfied God's wrath in your place, and His forgiveness and peace offered to you are true. The invitation is for you to humble yourself and to ask God to open your heart to Him. There is nothing more comforting than having the assurance of spending eternity in heaven after you die.

_____

_____

Cornel Rizea can be reached at **cornel@rizea-books.com**.

You can find out more at **www.rizea-books.com**.

www.ingramcontent.com/pod-product-compliance
Lightning Source LLC
LaVergne TN
LVHW011839060526
838200LV00054B/4105